Conte

Liber Al and the 50 Gates of Babalon by Steven Ashe	5
Aleister Crowley - Good Idea of the 20th century by Snoo Wilson	9
Liber Samekh and the Holy Guardian Angel By Shantidevi	16
How to do it	25
The attainment	29
Austin Osman Spare A Life in Pictures 1900-1956 By Robert Ansell	32
Enochian Magick By Steve Nicholls	37
Omphalus, Leyline, BNP house.	39
Magickal Squares of the Planets	44
Sound Workshop By Jan Fries	46
The Mysteries of Lam By Michael Staley	48
0. Introduction	48
1. Extra-terrestrialism	49
2. Origins of Lam	54
3. Future Directions	64
Cut Up and Collage in Magick By Dave Lee	66
BABALON By M C Medusa	70
BABALON as a New Aeon Deity	70
Working with Babalon	72
Babalon and Tantra.	74

Preface

Do what thou wilt shall be the whole of the law

Aleister Crowley may have died in 1947, but his influence is still very much felt by the magician of the new aeon. The CD soundtrack *The Beast Speaks* sold 8000 copies since its release in 1993, and the paperback edition of Crowley's *Confessions* was number two in Virgin Megastores top ten books. The modern magician is no slavish follower or member of some mind bending cult. Crowley's watch word was Thelema (The Crowleian pronunciation is Theh-LEE-mah, the accent being on the vowel of the second syllable, Greek speakers say the accent should be on the vowel of the first syllable for it to be pronounced right....ThEH-lee-mah) - which means [free] Will. Those who choose to follow this magical path aim to de-condition themselves, to develop independence of spirit and ultimately to become their very own self. One of the many attractions of Crowley's type of magick, was this advice to follow one's own way and create your own life path. You don't need a priest or a judge to tell you how to act - work it out for yourself.

As part of the process of developing self-knowledge, Crowley advocated the practice of magick. This he defined as 'the science and art of causing change in conformity with will.'

Thelemic magick can be either a *system* or an *approach* to the magick of any tradition, e.g. Hermetic, Ceremonial, even Witchcraft. In Thelema, as in all other styles of magick, there are two different types of magical organization - the 'Masonic' and the 'Rosicrucian'. The Masonic tends to be organized into definite hierarchical orders; whereas the Rosicrucian is more freeform, often a mere network of peers. The authors of what follows reflect many of these different styles of Thelemic magick and reading what they say is perhaps the best way to grasp what Thelemic magick is all about.

Mogg Morgan, Oxford, Lammas 2002

Love and do what you will

Thelemic Magick I

Being
the proceedings of the
Ninth International Symposium of
Thelemic Magick
22nd October 1994

Papers and workshops by
Snoo Wilson, Stephen Ashe,
Shantidevi, Robert Ansell, Michael
Staley, Jan Fries, Steve Nicholls,
Dave Lee, M C Medusa and
Svapnamatadevi

edited
by Mogg Morgan

Golden Dawn Publications

Second Edition © 1998 & 2002, OGDOS and various authors

All rights reserved. No part of this work may be reproduced or utilized in any form by any means electronic or mechanical, including *xerography, photocopying, microfilm*, and *recording,* or by any information storage system without permission in writing from the publisher.

ISBN   1869928-342

Published by
Mandrake of Oxford
PO Box 250
OXFORD
OX1 1AP (UK)

A CIP catalogue record for this book is available from the British Library and the US Library of Congress.

Liber Al and the 50 Gates of Babalon by Steven Ashe

Perhaps the greatest achievement of Crowley's esoteric career was his reception of the *Book of the Law* in Cairo, Egypt, April 1904. If he had not received this communication then we certainly wouldn't be sitting here now in tribute to his life and work.

I'm here to spend fifteen minutes talking with you about the *Book of the Law*; about its significance and revelations, but particularly about one key passage - verse 51 of the first chapter of the work.

First of all though let's pass two minutes or so in meditation upon the opening words of the *Book of the Law*.

[At this point an excerpt of the Nu Ordo Templi's audio recording of *Liber Al* was played to the audience: Chapter One, verses 1-15 inclusive]

We Thelemites believe the *Book of the Law* to be a genuine example of what is commonly termed channelling. In the case of the *Book of the Law* what was being channelled was the spirit of the age through a variety of archetypal personas associate with the Egyptian Gods.

The opening address of the conference

Thelemic magick I

Unlike many examples of channelling, the *Book of the Law* doesn't merely repeat to us knowledge of which we are already aware. It casts an interesting perspective upon mysteries associated with the western tradition. Take for example, verse fifty one of the first chapter.

[At this point the relevant verse was played to the audience from the audio cassette of Liber Al:]

'There are four gates to one palace. The floor of that palace is of silver and gold. Lapis Lazuli and jasper are there and all rare scents - jasmine and rose and the emblems of death...'

The 'four gates to one palace', referred to in this last quotation from the *Book of the Law*, is a reference to the Qabalistic system we refer to as the *Fifty gates of intelligence*. A system which, frankly, is overlooked by the majority of contemporary practitioners of the Qabalah.

Although vague references to the system of the fifty gates can be found in the *Zohar*, the only modern reference to it as a practical system is to be found in Wynn Westcott's translation of the *Sepher Yetzirah* in the form of a medieval speculative commentary which is practically useless as a key to understanding what the system is all about.

In fact, I believe that it is only in the light of the passage of the *Book of the Law* that we have just heard that any valid interpretation of the system of the fifty gates may be arrived at.

The number fifty has been demonstrated to be of special significance to a variety of esoteric doctrines. It occurs again and again in Robert Temple's *Sirius Mystery* where he makes continued specific references to the appearance of the number fifty in relation to ancient mythologies such as the *Epic of Gilgamesh* and the story of the Argonauts.

Thelemic magick I

Specifically Temple related the number fifty to the period of the binary star Sirius - a star which modern esotericists relate to the phantom sphere known as *Daath* upon the Qabalistic Tree of Life. In the system of the fifty gates as laid down in Westcott's translation of the *Sepher Yetzirah*, the fiftieth gate is related to the combined emanation of the second and third Sephiroth upon the Tree of Life - Chokmah and Binah. Because of this, we can attribute the fiftieth gate to the vortex within the Abyss we know as Daath. But why should this mysterious sephira be referred to as the fiftieth gate?

If one considers the Sephiroth upon the tree of life to be emanations of the primordial light above the tree - then each emanation may be thought to be composed of its own unique qualities. Each sephira on the tree of life contains something of the energy of each of the spheres above it. Because of this, we say that Chesed - the fourth sphere - is made of four gates: these gates are formed by the portions of essence lent to this sphere by the three spheres above it on the tree and the nature of the mystical experience associated with that sphere (in the case of Chesed - this would be love).

Thus, Malkuth - the tenth and lowest sphere upon the tree - can be thought of as being comprised of ten gates which lead to the palace of Yesod - the ninth sphere which comprises nine gates and so on.

When one has attuned oneself to each of the gates of the Sephiroth upon the tree up to and including Chesed - the fourth sephira - one will have passed through forty-nine gates in all. The three, uppermost Sephiroth known as the supernal triad cannot be accessed by humanity directly according to certain elements of the tradition because they exist above the world of Yetzirah - or formation, of which man in his present state is a part.

Therefore these Sephiroth can only be intuited through experience of the phantom sphere known as Daath, the *fiftieth gate* which bridges the worlds of formation (Yetzirah) and creation (Briah).

Thelemic magick I

[At this point a tape of *Liber Al* 2 verse 49 was played:]

'...This is of the four there is a fifth who is invisible and therein am I as a babe in an egg.'

The four gates to one palace are therefore the four experiences of the sphere of Chesed, akin to the gathering of the four grails in order to bring balance and harmony to the land.

The original place of Malkuth was that now thought to be occupied by the vortex of Daath. Thus the gathering of the 'four grail objects' familiar to those pursuing any Indo-European path will restore Malkuth 'reborn' to its proper place upon the tree - at least as far as the world view of the aspirant pursuing this system is concerned.

The earlier quotation we have heard from the *Book of the Law* has helped us to restore the system of the fifty gates to the tradition of the practical Qabalah. This is only one example of how the received text of *Liber Al* has cast light upon mysteries which may hitherto have been obscured by indifference or misunderstanding.

I will leave you now with some parting words from the *Book of the Law*.

[A tape was then played of *Liber Al* 3 verse 58]

'There is no law beyond Do what thou wilt.......'

Aleister Crowley - *Good Idea* of the 20th century by Snoo Wilson

Snoo Wilson is a writer and broadcaster and author of *The Number of the Beast* a play about Crowley's life. The text of his talk at the symposium is not available but here is the script of his recent television broadcast for *Channel Four*.

The charge of Satanism levied on the shade of the notorious drug-fiend and author Aleister Crowley has not gone away, half a century after his death. Satanism is the worship of Satan or Sha'itan, the Hebrew word for adversary. So what then did he do that was so very very bad? Crowleyanity's catchphrase was 'Do What thou Wilt shall be the whole of the Law', a parody of St Augustine's 'Love and do what thou wilt'. Augustine was from Numibia, and repented his excesses. Crowley was from Leamington in Warwickshire and regretted very little.

The Beaverbrook newspapers christened Mr Crowley 'The Wickedest Man in the World.' Tabloid satanism however is still a serious charge even if the theology behind the charge is cloudy. It is not helped by his first biographer, informative, but spiteful. Later on, in the sixties, Crowley appears on the cover of *Sergeant Pepper*, between Mae West and an oriental guru, but a whiff of sulphur and brimstone still clings to the name - an achievement in our pseudo-secular age.

When young, Crowley belonged briefly to the magical society,

Thelemic magick I

the Hermetic Order of the Golden Dawn, along with W B Yeats. But unable to brook chastity or competition for long, the bully-boy of British magic appeared in the inner sanctum, dressed in a kilt, playing the bagpipes. Crowley was duly expelled from the order, pinched a number of rituals and started his own. Disgraceful but hardly diabolic.

Crowley was a Victorian. His strongest and most modern actions were taken against the spirit of the age.

I do not wish to paint Crowley as a saint, nor do I think he is the reverse. 'Queen Victoria' AC wrote, 'was sheer suffocation, a vast thick fog that enveloped us all. We could not breathe, we could not see, the spirit of her age had killed everything we cared for.' He certainly never sacrificed his offspring. The Beast liked to boast of having murdered thousands of his sons, but this was nothing more than a late Victorian joke about the fate of his semen after masturbation. Masturbation, Crowley believed, could be sacred, an operation of the ninth degree, as he termed it. Today the Catholic Church, while not going all nine degrees of the way, have made a start.

Luckily we don't have to go all the way with AC to recognise the value of the kindred disciplines he explored in the unconscious. Astrology and the *I Ching* are just two of the esoterica that he championed that are now in the commonwealth of knowledge.

The Beast was brought up in religious dread, in a house rife with the idea of Satanism, and later reacted against it with all the force of his considerable personality. As for the visions that he or his partners went into during extended sessions, I cannot accept the record of Crowley's various encountered entities as that much separate from him. Be they his Holy Guardian Angel, Aiwass, or lower down the spiritual scale, they all seemed to possess a giveaway trace of their dreamer's broad brush-strokes.

Crowley liked sex and drugs. Lots of drugs. Ether, alcohol, Anhanolium Lewinii, opium, and its derivatives cocaine and heroin.

Thelemic magick I

The speed with which Crowley's successive wives and consorts fell into degeneracy and alcoholism was remarkable as the Beast, codename 'Frater Perdurabo - I will endure' - trudged on in his mission to save the world. Certainly Crowley preyed on the weak. To trample his loved ones into the primordial slime became a sort of Nietzschean imperative for Crowley. Indulgence in coke and heroin play their part as ever in this kind of destructive egotistic behaviour. Opiates were freely available over the counter for the first fifty years of the Beast's life. Aspiring junkies should take note of the connection between loss of libido and drug abuse, in his intensely self-scrutinising diaries. Chastening thought, hardly diabolic.

If Crowley was not a Satanist, and not a saint, then what was he? Gerald Yorke was a sometime disciple and told me he thought Crowley, who he called 'Old Crow' was a failed magus. Gerald had a talisman, made from dried semen and menstrual blood on paper, created along Crowleyan lines and he had consecrated this talisman with the aim of magically drawing together all of Crowley's manuscripts. The operation, he said, had been successful. Gerald seemed a nice old man, and not at all diabolical. He gave me Old Crow's magic wand to hold. The wand was of heavy brass, and had been shortened to two foot for an invocation. I gingerly examined the shortened end, which had been chamfered crudely on a lathe. Then I gave it back to Gerald, who announced to me with a patrician giggle, 'If you had dropped it I wouldn't have had anything more to do with you.'

In the early days Crowley had a private income. In later years, when he lived off his disciples, he does not appear to have abated his roaring persona, testing the limits of social behaviour by biting unlucky women on the back of the hand to draw blood - Mr Crowley's unforgettable serpent kiss - sometimes by cooking inedibly hot curries - oh, that Mr Crowley has done it again - or slyly defecating on the rugs of his hostesses, to tell them...What, exactly,

Thelemic magick I

are you trying to say, 666? But when up against the nuclear merchants and other genocide enthusiasts of the twentieth century, gross social behaviour seems a quibble. And does not the Master Gurdjieff say, 'Always astonish?' Gurdjieff, who bought and sold carpets to keep his harem going, couldn't stand AC and on their one meeting the Turkish sage told him 'Get out, you dirty inside.' What had AC done? Parked one of his brown Beelzebubs on a priceless rug? As a rule, Maguses do not get on.

Crowley on his drive to save the world had taken up an oriental tantric process for concentrating the wish during the moment of orgasm. In Tantra it is called the left hand way. Crowley called it sex magic. The wish according to devotees, will get you what you need, not everything you ask for. There is a school of thought that suggests that he was the first sex instructor of the twentieth century, but if he occupies this position, it is by default, as sex explorer is closer to the mark, supping on the juices of himself and his companion of choice, for their rejuvenative powers. He was in his seventies, plagued with asthma, when he died, so it is not clear whether Dr Crowley's special formula worked, or not.

Another of the charges levelled against Crowley is that he was once a German spy. It is true that he wrote for German newspapers when he lived in New York during the first world war. He had run out of money living in Manhattan. The Beast, tongue as ever in his own cheek, when it wasn't up someone else's, wrote deliberately wild propaganda for a pro-German magazine, even giving his aunt's suburban address as a target. If his aunt forgave him, we should.

Three snapshots of things which actually happened at that same time. Old Crow doing coke, writing potboilers at 5,000 words a day, to keep his commune afloat. D H Lawrence's books, the subsequent staple of spotty teenagers, are burnt by the public hangman. And Lawrence's nude self-portraits, the frontline challenging Victorian values, are being seized from a London gallery. Today Lawrence has long been rehabilitated as a voice of sanity, in spite of his frequent silliness. But Old Crow, diabolical druggie, is still to return from outer darkness and the place of wailing and gnashing of teeth.

Crowley was bisexual and well after his first marriage to Rose Kelly, he had an affair with the poet Victor Neuberg, during which Crowley behaved badly as usual. Indeed most men and women who drew close enough to share the Beast's embrace ended up reviling him, for his egotism left little room for lengthy friendship. (Deirdre McClellan, who encountered him after his bankruptcy in 1935 was a rare exception.)

Montague, the seventh earl of Tankerville, bravely hired AC, The Logos of the Aeon, to rid him of witchcraft. The commoner Crowley, forever attempting to hurl himself beyond mere Lords and royalty, to godhead, was finally rumbled by his paranoid, titled patient. The Earl's last words to our magus were memorable. 'I'm sick of your teaching, teaching, teaching, as if you were God almighty, and I were a poor bloody shit in the street.'

More than anything, Crowley was a victim of the rise of the popular newspapers. In the 1920s when Crowley was living in Sicily, D H Lawrence, that other monster, was living over the other side of Etna from Old Crow. Lawrence of course had ran off with the cousin of a German fighter ace. Like Crowley, he was not only sexually obsessed, but downright unpatriotic. They could have met, they didn't, but history can be rewritten in the movie. A walk-on part for Lawrence, foxy and hirsute, peering out at his shaven headed rival from a post office queue in Cefalu, watching the swirl of Crowley's purple cape, as he strides past like a cold Roman Emperor in the sun to keep an appointment with destiny, which happens to be himself.

It was not in fact Beaverbrook and the British gutter press that finally destroyed the Logos of the Aeon's uneasy love-nest. Benito Mussolini would brook no oppostion and banned secret societies in Italy. Old Crow, who in his time had joined more Masonic Lodges than he had trouser-legs to roll, was given a week to leave. One of

Thelemic magick I

Crowley's guests, a brilliant mathematician who was in Crowley's thrall, had earlier died from enteritis. Crowley naturally was blamed in the papers for the death of a disciple, and returned to England a public scoundrel, a position he deliberately misunderstood for fame.

In 1904, Crowley had dictated to his wife a tract which he subsequently came to believe was going to replace the *Bible*. The *Book Of the Law* is full of obscure injunctions, such as 'Build me a fortress! dung it about with enginery of war!' But compared to the direct results of *Mein Kampf*, composed fifteen years later, the results of the *Book of the Law* can hardly be called satanic, though it does owe a deal to the deliberately archaic language of the King James *Bible*.

The Beast's insouciance and sexual panache was styled on Lord Byron, though the later poet had to invent any titles he wanted. And invent 666 did, a whole pseudo-aristocratic wardrobe: Baron Svaroff, the Laird of Boleskine, the Ipsissimus, a magical grade, the very thing itself. He died broke in a boarding house in Hastings in 1947, and the 'Hymn to Pan', a fine poem by him, was read at his funeral.

More of the Beast's purple prose is in print and on the lips of the young now than ever before. He would have said, 'I told you so.' It was Crowley's rival, the poet Yeats, whose verbal magic was soaked in Golden Dawn symbolism who should have the last word. He wrote:

somewhere in the sands of the desert.
A shape with lion body and head of a man,
A gaze blank and pitiless as the sun,
Is moving its slow thighs, while all about it
Reel shadows of the indignant desert birds
....
And what rough beast, its hour come round at last,
Slouches towards Bethlehem to be born?

Thelemic magick I

Penned in 1921, the lines have been taken as foreshadowing the West's collapse into fascism. It could describe the Beast, trying to live up to the impossible absolute of the bleak poetic marvel that was his vision and inspiration as well as Yeats. Life, not Satan let Crowley down. Yeats is right though. Today, love him or loathe him, the Beast's hour is coming round at last. Drugs, sexual excess, anarchy and egotism - a true mirror for our times. A movie of the Beast is overdue.

'Love is the Law, Love under Will.'

Snoo's novel *I, Crowley, almost the last confession of the beast.* is publiushed by Mandrake.

Snoo Wilson Feb 94

Liber Samekh and the Holy Guardian Angel By Shantidevi

This talk is about Guardian spirits, and in particular what has been known as the Holy Guardian Angel. Many years ago I went to a similar talk at the Oxford Golden Dawn Occult Society, and I got hold of a copy of the *Sacred Magic of Abra-Melin the Mage*, to which the speaker kept referring. However, the text of the book went over my head so I forgot about the subject for a couple of years until I heard a talk in Oxford by Maggie Ingalls from the Ma'at network. She spoke about the Aeon of Ma'at and I found much of what she was discussing extremely inspiring; sadly however she stipulated that in order to work Ma'at magick you had to have first obtained the Knowledge and Conversation of your Holy Guardian Angel. So I thought it was about time I got this HGA business over with so I could get on to the really interesting work which was Ma'at magick. I plunged straight in to the invocation of the Angel, and I've been doing it ever since. I've decided that the invocation of one's Holy Guardian Angel is one of the most important magickal operations there are, one of the few things that are really worth doing, and is in fact one of the meanings of life!

What do I mean by a Holy Guardian Angel? There are many names which have been given to it. They include: daimon (which incidentally comes from a Greek word meaning 'deity' and only later became 'demonised')

Thelemic magick I

inner genius
higher self
guiding spirit
divine spark
true will
agathodaimon

Some people would also associate the Holy Guardian Angel with a spirit guide. I think that the term 'spirit guide' is used so liberally now that it often seems to relate to any inner planes contact - I would rather use one of the terms above. The Holy Guardian Angel, as I see it, is, a personal and individual guardian spirit. I would also identify it as the True Will.

This talk will look at, firstly, what the Holy Guardian Angel is, what HGA magick is like. I will attempt to answer questions like: what does invoking the HGA mean? Many writers talk of obtaining *Knowledge and Conversation* of the Holy Guardian Angel - what does this mean? Why bother with this kind of magick at all? Finally, how do you achieve it? I will look at one method in detail. Because this talk is intensely personal there will be many references to my own experience. I have to say that I have not achieved the full Knowledge and Conversation of my angel yet - however, there are things which have helped me get to the stage where I now am, and I'll mention some of them in passing.

So: what is the Holy Guardian Angel? The idea of an individual guardian spirit goes back thousands of years and is important in two of the major influences on modern ritual magick: ancient Greece, and Jewish mysticism.

In ancient Greece, the Platonic school discussed in detail the philosophy of 'daimonology' because there was a tradition which described Socrates as being visited by a 'daimon'. Socrates talked of hearing an 'inner voice'. Generally this voice had an inhibiting effect, warning Socrates against taking the wrong course of action. The 'daimon' may also have been connected with epileptic fits - Socrates suffered from epilepsy. Whether or not Socrates himself

Thelemic magick I

actually thought of that 'inner voice' as a kind of guardian spirit, Georg Luck[1] says, is unclear (his accusers called it a 'strange god', hence the charge of impiety made against Socrates). However, in the *Republic* (5th century BC) Plato describes 'guardian daemons' who accompany a man through life, know his innermost thoughts, his most secret actions, and, after death, act as his advocates or accusers before the throne of judgement. By the Hellenistic period, (from the third century BC onwards), the belief in a kind of guardian angel, a good daemon or 'agathodaimon', had become fairly common. According to legend, the pagan philosopher Plotinus had his angel invoked for him by a priest in Rome (he was an Egyptian priest at the temple of Isis - which was, according to him, the only pure place in the city!). The priest was reputedly astonished at what a great and noble soul Plotinus had. At this time some also believed in an 'evil spirit' (kakodaimon), but this wasn't universal.

(Interestingly Crowley proposed that his followers should use the term 'kakodaimon' when they met an evil spirit, in particular a Christian priest. They were, he said, to cry 'apo pantos kakodaimonos' (get away from me all evil). Whether Crowley himself had the bottle to do this is unclear. In *Remembering Aleister Crowley* Kenneth Grant recalls when as a young, hot-blooded disciple he quoted this at a priest in the street, in Crowley's company. Crowley was hideously embarrassed and told Grant to stop!)

The other important idea-stream comes from Jewish mysticism, and in particular, the Abra-Melin magickal system. This has a long history, but very briefly: *The Sacred Magic of Abra-Melin the Mage* was written in 1458 by Abraham the Jew. The story goes that Abraham searched around the world for many years for the True Magic. Finally he found Abra-Melin who was living as a hermit in the desert in a small town near the Nile. He instructed Abraham in the magic - and Abraham performed it with considerable success, apparently between the years of around 1409-1458. (He was also, it seems, involved in all sorts of intrigues in the European Court at the same time). The basic idea is as follows:

Thelemic magick I

Every individual has a Guardian Angel and a malevolent demon. In the wider universe, all material phenomena are created as the result of the actions of evil spirits who are under the control of good ones. The idea is that by prayer and contemplation in a suitable place you can call forth your HGA who will instruct you in the right use of the demons; hence in the Abra-Melin operation there are talismans to be consecrated for such purposes as bringing the dead back to life, getting gold, flying through the air, etc. There are many instructions for these things. The idea is that you can do any of these things but only if you've achieved the knowledge and conversation of the HGA!

So, the central idea is clear enough: you have in some form an inner genius. Most magicians believe that you can contact this, through magick. But just as importantly, it makes clear that you can only work these other 'miracles' once you have made contact with your angel. Just making the talismans and muttering the magick words is not enough. As DuQuette[2] puts it, in order to have god-like powers you must first become god.

I think that it is the contacting of this inner genius through magick that makes magick different from religion because central to the individual's spiritual life is the contacting of an individual, personal guardian spirit, through one's own efforts and not mediated through any other priesthood. This form of magick, this individual gnosis, is also qualitatively different from most of the other magickal operations we do - like celebrating pagan weddings and funerals, fire festivals, results magick, etc. It is a different kind of experience altogether.

So, we have established what the Holy Guardian Angel is. But why contact your Angel anyway?

Maggie Ingalls in an unpublished book on Ma'at Magick[3] describes contact with the Angel as giving a true sense of purpose, 'clear vision of the shape of your work and a satisfaction and joy in the doing of it.' I think this is a worthy explanation, but would add to it the sheer ecstasy of the magickal experience of any contact with your angel. From my experience it's also very emotional and often accompanied with indescribable bliss! Here is, for instance, an extract from the magickal diary of Victor Neuburg, a disciple of Crowley, who performed the Abra-Melin operation while on a retreat with Crowley at Boleskine:

> I then became a green triangle (apex upwards) in a violet crown or circle, then a blazing comet flaming in the hair of a God; then a flaming star. After this I became absorbed in and identified with white light. This experience was accompanied by extreme ecstasy.
>
> I found myself at the Court of Horus (he was jet-black), who gave me two tablets inscribed INRI and TARO respectively.... Horus sent me out to gaze at the clear blue heavens, wherein were myriads of stars...[4]

An extraordinary and inspiring vision!

The root idea is that obtaining the Knowledge and Conversation of your Holy Guardian Angel - that is making a real contact with it - will enable us to know our true will and to do it, thereby understanding the true meaning of 'do what thou wilt shall be the whole of the law'. Most of us currently have a sense of self that is nothing more than a mask, a persona, a collection of impulses, feelings, emotions and images of ourselves which pull in conflicting directions. By contacting our Holy Guardian Angel we become united with our true self, we achieve clarity of vision instead of being constantly dissipated in inner conflicts. So it seems that although now we 'see in a glass darkly' we will then see clearly. Another analogy would be the restoring of an Eden - I personally think that the myth of the Fall is probably related to our sense of separateness from our true wills, our secret self beyond self. By contacting our angel we also regain Eden. Tantalising stuff!

It is hardly surprising then that obtaining Knowledge and Conversation of the Holy Guardian Angel is seen by most magicians as *the* magickal operation, in fact, the Great Work itself. Crowley goes one step further and says that as 'you have no right but to do

Thelemic magick I

your will' and that any other magickal operation which deviates from this 'vertical straight line upwards' towards your angel tends to be the stuff of black magick! In *Magick* the one who has attained HGA is variously described as someone who isn't fooled in their visions and who doesn't need to spend their whole lives checking them in *777*; someone who is 'no less than the co-heir of gods, a Lord of Light...conscious of his own consecrated course, and confidently ready to run it'. Who can't fail to be inspired by this idea? Little wonder then that magicians seem to look to the attainment of HGA with the same fervid expectation of an adolescent getting their first sexual experience.

Even more compelling is the idea that your angel has in fact been with you since the beginning. The best known ritual for invoking the angel is called the 'Bornless One' - one of the ideas behind this being that the angel was not created nor will it ever be destroyed. Maggie Ingalls writes that it has 'been waiting for you all your life; yearning for you, watching out for you, courting you in a thousand subtle ways'; Crowley writes that once you start practising magick you are on a road inexorably leading towards the Great Work - even if you originally got interested in magick because you wanted to make money or get lots of sexual partners. It was certainly the way with me - although I won't tell you what my original intentions were!

So...we want union with the angel and the angel wants union with us. And I think it's important to bear in mind that you are probably closer to your angel than you think, even if you have not yet invoked it or even had a vision of it. The very fact that you practise magick is a signal to your angel of your aspiration. And many of the workings that you are now doing are relevant. For instance, when you perform the pentagram rite you say the lines 'for about me flames the pentagram/And in the column shines the six-rayed star'. That six-rayed star is a symbol of the angel: two triangles, one pointing upwards, one downwards, represents the angel as the mediator between the seen and the unseen, the 'begetter and manifester into the light'. Whenever I perform this ritual I imagine

Thelemic magick I

the my 'six-rayed star initiator' above me and then meditate for a minute on my angel pouring himself forth within my soul, before I continue the rite.

What is the next step? Traditionally, there are two stages to the attainment. The first is a vision of the angel. Sometimes this happens spontaneously, perhaps while involved in another ritual. I know when it happened to me I was doing a meditation upon the Egyptian God Set and was pathworking in the desert. (Interestingly at the time I was tired of practising magick and was going to give it another year; then, if nothing happened, I would pack it in and spend my time doing something else. What's also interesting is that I since discovered that there's an important link between Set and HGA magick. In any case this experience was entirely unexpected.) The vision was of a being of light of huge size - utterly awe-inspiring, fearsome, like a kind of divine grace; I never forgot myself so completely. There was a sense of being utterly insignificant. Anyway, when the vision faded I was left with the angel's name and of course a burning desire to repeat the experience. You're probably asking why I didn't use the experience more and perhaps even ask questions but at the time I was so overwhelmed it would have been impossible.

The second stage is the attainment of Knowledge and Conversation of the angel. This is a more profound experience of it, and implies being possessed by the spirit of the angel. A parallel I like is that the vision is like realising that you have inherited an immense fortune. But taking possession of that fortune, experiencing it fully, is like attaining knowledge and conversation of the angel. This takes the form of an invocation - most magicians decide to go for Liber Samekh in Crowley's *Magick in Theory and Practice*, of which more later. There are in fact other ways! Crowley himself says that in the A\A\ they did not insist that people use this ritual although it was used with success by some of Crowley's colleagues.

I think there are several features of any HGA invocation, however:

Thelemic magick I

1. 'Inflame yourself in prayer'. This isn't difficult when you consider what a major magickal rite this is and what the attributes of the angel are. DuQuette suggests you should be like a lovesick person, constantly thinking of the object of your desire. I can understand this - I've performed the rite in my sleep before. The more you work with the angel the more burning your desire is. Crowley himself is said to have performed the invocation astrally while travelling across China and falling, without realising it, over a small cliff! The hard thing about the rite is that traditionally magick doesn't work if done with too much 'lust of result'. I find it almost impossible to do the ritual without lust of result! And lust is the operative word here - my remark about adolescent sex wasn't entirely flippant; the imagery in HGA work is often very sexual, (as indeed in any invocation where you are trying to achieve union with the divine) and the ecstasy and self-surrender is definitely sexual.

2. 'Invoke often' The tradition was, you went away for six months and performed the rite once a day for the first month, twice for the second, three times for the third, four times a day in the fourth month, and then for two months, constantly. In Crowley's *Magick*, he suggests that the entire rite should take *eleven* months, with the eleventh moon 'consecrated wholly to this Work; let him be instant in continual ardour, dismissing all but his sheer needs to eat and sleep.' Some people have withdrawn from the world in this way. Others have simply tried to perform the rite as often as they can, while going about their working lives. I originally decided to take this latter course because as so often there's never a good time to start and I thought it best just to try to overcome fear and inertia and get going. I have been performing the ritual for about three years - not every day, not even always every week, but fairly consistently I'm not sure if it's the best way, but it's a way. The most important thing is just that you go ahead and do it. The forces you are invoking anyway are so strong that I think they will in time create the necessary conditions. In any case you have to dig yourself in for a

long haul, I think!

3. Make the Oath. Doing the Bornless one rite is very unsettling. It also requires a great deal of mental and physical energy. And sometimes the idea of carrying on until you succeed is daunting. Crowley's motto of 'Perdurabo' - 'I shall endure to the end' is useful here. There have been occasions when, I have heard myself almost screaming with frustration the line from the invocation, 'come forth most hidden light!' At times you have to do anything you can do regain your motivation. Everyone who has written about it seems to agree that the Oath is necessary.

4. Get assistance. This ritual isn't set apart from all your other magickal work. It may be that there are deities or angels or spirits who have helped you before: I have recently started saying a prayer to Ganesha, the destroyer of obstacles, asking for help before the ritual, and for me at least, I believe Ma'at holds the key to the attainment. Other people have suggested making a talisman to the archangel Michael, or a prayer to Ra-Hoor-Kuit.

5. Prepare properly. Traditionally this meant retreating from the world, building a special oratory, fasting and praying. I think the importance of these actions are symbolic; they all symbolise the aspirant's wish to be 'one-pointed', to have 'one star in sight', and not to be distracted. They also symbolise the focus of the ritual, where integration with the angel leads to a state where you're not constantly being torn apart by different and often unconscious emotions and impulses. Maggie suggests 'vigorous self-assessment, writing out the story of one's life, hopes, dreams, aspirations, etc'. Thelemites tend to shy away from this because it sounds sissy, although Crowley suggests also a similar course of action. It's probably worth doing. And of course you need some experience of invocation! *Liber Astarte* or a similar devotional practice to a deity, is a useful precursor to *Samekh* and helps to build the intensity of

feeling you need.

How to do it
As I said, there are other ways to achieve this, but I will focus on this one rite.

Liber Samekh
What is it? *The Bornless One Rite* comes from the preliminary invocation of the Goetia (a word which means 'howling' and which refers to a system of magick which involves using many strange-sounding and barbarous names). It is based upon the translation by C W Goodwin of a *Graeco-Egyptian work on Magick*. Goodwin translated it as the 'headless' one. The 'Headless One' was a name given (by the Gnostics) to the Sun in Amenti, ie the light in the underworld, represented by a decapitated figure and paralleled by the Egyptian image of a lioness or maneless lion. The idea is that the sun here is 'feminine' phase of passivity and darkness, like the lion shorn of its mane yet fierce with concealed force and hidden heat. The image is of the secret self, the hidden God submerged below the horizon, like the sun in the underworld or like (in a vision I had) a goldmine in a dark hillside! Throughout the ritual the solar imagery, the secret, spiritual sun, is paramount, as you would expect in a rite that pertains to Tiphareth, the solar sphere on the Tree of Life.

The first paragraph is very interesting. Firstly, the name 'Liber Samekh', and secondly the sentence just beneath it 'Congressues Cum Daemone'. It is called *Liber Samekh* but its real title should be Liber Samael. There was typically a reluctance to utter godnames too frequently which is why in the old testament the name of God was represented by the four letters rather than spelling out the name itself. Similarly, rather than constantly say the name of Samael it is abbreviated to Samekh. Interestingly, Samekh is traditionally not an angel or god at all but a demon, in fact one of the most high-ranking demons who led the rebellion which got the angels thrown out of

Thelemic magick I

heaven. Gershom Sholem in his book *Kabbalah* devotes a whole chapter to him but some of the most interesting points about Samekh are:

1. He is viewed as the demonic aspect of the element of fire just as Michael is the angelic aspect. This is interesting because many sources describe the HGA as 'the voice of fire'.

2. He is described as deriving his name from the word *sami* meaning 'blind'. This I think is relevant because a lot of the imagery in Liber Samekh is of the angel as a secret sun, of a hidden light.

3. He is supposed to have planted the vine that caused the fall of Adam and therefore was cursed and became Satan. This is critical: Samekh is the bestower of secret knowledge.

4. He is supposed to be the guardian angel of all the nations except for Israel. Michael is the Angel of Israel. There is a constant fight between the two of them which will only end at the end of the world when Samekh will be taken in shackles to Israel. This image surely has a parallel in the conflict between the Egyptian gods Horus and Set.

The bit about the congress with demons is interesting too: there is a paradox at work here. You're invoking your Angel and yet you're getting visited by all these demons! Without getting too hysterical, lots of strands of thought about what angels and demons are have to be teased apart.

Quite often when you first perform the ritual you start hearing strange noises on the edge of the circle which make the hairs at the back of your neck stand on end. It's worth thinking through what you think demons are, as there's no doubt that you encounter some when performing the rite and in dreams afterwards. I personally think that they represent unresolved tensions and conflicts within

Thelemic magick I

you and that they're as real as anything else in this universe. Traditionally you had to evoke the demons once you had attained knowledge of your Angel, and bind them to your Will; the assumption being that your angel is mightier than any of these and will help you to integrate these parts of your personality. The tricky thing is that when you invoke the Angel, as it approaches, so do the demons; the inner tensions become more unbearable.

Another way of looking at it is that the rite is all about the world in its entirety. It posits a world created by your angel purely for the purpose of self-realisation; the first attribute of the Angel in the Bornless one is 'thou that didst create the Earth and the Heavens', suggesting that everything, whether it's traditionally an angel or a demon, is part of the world which the angel has created, and that everything is interconnected. It's worth bearing in mind too that Samekh is the legendary angel that gives us knowledge; that the Greek word 'daimon' from which we get the word 'demon' originally just meant 'divine being'; and that many spirits, gods, and angels became demonized by other cultures and traditions. Think how the Christians have demonized Shaitan, or Pan. And finally, most of us believe that 'there is no part of me which is not of the gods'; as a tantrik I delight in all impurity; so just because the rite is called Liber Samekh and involves congress with demons *is no reason not to do it.*

So, we have a rite which involves experiences viewed as both highly dangerous and yet eminently desirable!

Before I go on to the ritual itself, I would like to add that Crowley changed the rite substantially. He used the term 'bornless' one because the True Will is not born, nor does it die. He also changed many of the barbarous names to include ancient godnames, many of which are explained in his commentary. Finally, he changed the parts which refer to the practitioner; originally the practitioner would identify with Moses but he changed the line from 'I am Moshe thy prophet, unto whom Thou didst commit Thy Mysteries, the Ceremonies of Israel' he changed the prophet's name to Ankh-f-n-

Thelemic magick I

Khonsu and substituted Khem (Egypt) for Israel'. You might want to change this again, if you don't want to identify with Crowley's magickal name, and you could substitute 'Thelema' for 'Khem'. Also it's advisable to substitute the name of your angel, if you know it, for the name given in the text. When I first performed the rite I thought it was absolutely sacrosanct and must stand exactly as it is - this is of course absolutely pointless. I think you have to adapt it.

The rite consists of three parts.

Preliminary invocation

Firstly, after performing the banishing, you call upon the angel, listing its attributes, invoking it as 'myself made perfect', and asserting your right to invoke it. You vibrate the barbarous names as powerfully as you can.

Elemental invocations

Then, you invoke each element in turn, vibrating the barbarous names with as much force and fire as you can muster. You can also recite the English lines which are attempts to paraphrase the godname. It's actually very difficult to do the rite without hyperventilating, there's so much of it.[5] At the same time you fling your consciousness outside the circle in each direction in turn, with each word pushing it further out - Crowley of course, suggests you imagine it like a phallus growing longer and longer, each time twice as long as the previous time, as you vibrate the names! You also visualize that elemental force whether as a lion, sea-serpent, etc, in the far, far distance, glowing in coloured light. Then, suddenly, you withdraw your consciousness back into yourself, gathering in as you do the full spiritual force of the element, so that the entire element in all its forms is concentrated within you, purifying and strengthening you. You have an awesome sense of the vast size, the entirety of everything. You can imagine the full force of the element's impact upon you: for instance when you invoke water ask for it to wash away the impurities in you that prevent the angel's approach. For

Thelemic magick I

earth, imagine the power of that element aiding you in physically manifesting your angel.

Once you have extended your consciousness and then contracted it again you repeat the 'chorus' or Charge: 'Hear me, and make all Spirits subject unto me, so that every spirit of the firmament and of the ether, on the earth and under the earth, on dry land and in water, of whirling air and rushing fire, and may every spell and scourge of God be obedient unto me.' The idea here is that you have an understanding of the harmony of all things; that you see everything as 'contributory causes of yourself'. I originally balked at this Charge, seeing it as the traditional gloomy, tight-arsed ceremonial magician trying to control all things. Not so! It is more to do with everything being interconnected, all part of the world the angel has created in order for it to manifest in you.

You repeat this for each element. When reading the ritual, several things strike you; the very sexual imagery - you have the sense that sexual desire is *the* driving force of the universe, that everything is in constant flux, constant motion; again the sense of the world in its entirety - there are so many strange images, so many contradictions, such rich imagery. It's too much to get your head around - one of the functions of the rite is I think to occupy the intellect so as to distract it from the main focus of the ritual which is becoming so perfectly attuned to the vibration of your angel that it is attracted to you. A parallel might be the meditation upon a Zen Buddhist koan - a paradoxical statement which is so strange, so complex, so contradictory that it breaks through the rational mind.

When you invoke spirit you don't withdraw the consciousness back inside you but visualize it as continually extended while continuing to invoke the angel with ever increasing fire and passion and intense aspiration, until you finally achieve the contact.

The attainment

Crowley includes detailed instructions for how to receive the angel; at first the ecstasy is too much to bear and you can just be overwhelmed by the sensation. Later, he says, by 'refining your rapture' it is possible to begin to ask questions of the angel instead of simply losing yourself in the experience. I don't know if this is possible - I haven't achieved it yet.

I will however continue performing the rite until this is achieved. In the time I have been practising it the thing I have found of most use is my magickal diary. I think I would have given up a long time ago if it had not been for this; over time you get insights and understanding of visions that you can never comprehend as they occur; it helps you to change the ritual as you need to and it is constantly encouraging. In the days after I have performed the rite my inner life is different; my dreams are different - all the evidence is there.

To summarize then, the invoking of the Holy Guardian Angel is one of the major aims of magick. Much much more has been written about results magick than ever about this very profound, very personal, utterly inspiring magickal experience, but I would say to everyone that you should try it. Don't let the fact that you can't take six months off and retreat from the world deflect you - you can always do what I have done and start in your own time. Don't worry if you don't know all the words of the ritual yet - you learn them soon enough as you do them. Whatever you do in your magickal work, don't neglect the invocation of your guardian spirit.

Can I finish by quoting the business card of a friend of mine? Under his name and address it reads 'wishing you speedy attainment of HGA'. I wish the same for you.

Further reading
Crowley, *Liber ABA Magick*, (Weisers 1995)
M Staley's article in this volume
I Regardie, *Ceremonial Magic* (Aquarian 1980)
DuQuette, *The Magick of Thelema* (Weiser 1994)

Notes

[1] Georg Luck, *Arcana Mundi* (Crucible 1987)
[2] Don Milo DuQuette, *The Magick of Thelema*, (Weiser 1994)
[3] Happily, soon to be published by Weisers
[4] Jean Overton Fuller, *The Magical Dilemma of Victor Neuburg* (Mandrake of Oxford 1990)
[5] Some people suggest you perform the rite entirely astrally but I have always had to vibrate the names and recite the invocations.

Austin Osman Spare
A Life in Pictures 1900-1956
By Robert Ansell

Having been asked to convey the contents of a slide lecture with the comparatively inadequate medium of the written word I have decided to dodge the issue. This then is most definitely *not* an attempt to bring to the absent reader a chronological account of Spare's life and graphic *oeuvre* in the way I very much enjoyed presenting it at the convivial 1994 Oxford Thelemic Symposium. Rather, I hope in this brief essay to illustrate why Gavin Semple and I became involved so heavily with Spare's work, provide also a thumb-nail sketch of Spare's life, and finally once again underline why Spare is one of the most important sorcerers of the twentieth century.

Although we had both been interested in Spare's life since the mid 1980s Gavin and I only met in 1989. Back in '86 the sole published biographical material available was through the innovative, but scarce *Images and Oracles of Austin Osman Spare* and 'Typhonian Trilogies' of Kenneth Grant. We decided that in order to understand Spare more fully a solid biographical foundation was an absolute necessity, and the last eight years pain-staking research have been devoted to this end. In addition to the biographical archive is our photo-library for Spare's graphic work. This forms a permanent record of his picture output, providing a working base for slide lectures, our planned biography and other future publications.

Thelemic magick I

Readers with original artwork by AOS may consider allowing access for us to photograph them for the archive, and any offers will be warmly welcomed. In 1992 Gavin and I published *The Witches' Sabbath* and *Axiomata* by AOS under the imprint of FULGUR, our modest publishing concern devoted to the Current. Two months after publication nearly 700 of the 1000 copies printed were accidentally pulped when our printer went bankrupt - making the book even rarer than some of Spare's earliest titles! Despite this unpleasant evocation of Choronzon, FULGUR has survived and is planning some amazing titles for 1995-1996. A disturbing sketchbook by AOS entitled *The Book of Ugly Ecstasy* and a new edition of *The Book of Pleasure* with footnotes on Spare's magical techniques and biography of the period will be appearing soon. Those still unfamiliar with Spare's work will wonder why he gets so much attention, so now I'll move on to the thumb-nail résumé.

Born in the City of London in 1886, Spare displayed an extraordinary ability for drawing. When his family moved to Kennington he came under the influence of 'Witch Patterson', who was to later initiate him onto the sorcerous path. As his art improved he was enrolled for evening classes at Lambeth Art School and in 1902 became the youngest ever recipient of the National Mathematics Award with his treatise on Solid Geometry. The following year he was recommended for a free scholarship to the Royal College of Art, and within two years a small drawing executed when he was only fourteen excited great interest amongst connoisseurs and art critics at the 1904 Royal Academy Summer Exhibition. Encouraged by success he privately published his first illustrated book *Earth Inferno* in February 1905 aged eighteen. A powerful and metaphysical perception of the 'self' in relation to the cosmos, *Earth Inferno* sought to communicate the fundamental principles of Spare's magical development, his personal gnosis, and heralded an active period of patronage and book illustration work. Art connoisseurs such as Charles Ricketts, André Rafflovich, Pickford Waller and Desmond Coke were quick to appreciate Spare's unique gift: the

Thelemic magick I

hand of Dürer and the eye of Dante. A second folio, *The Book of Satyrs*, was privately published in 1907 - just prior to his first notorious West End exhibition at the Bruton Gallery in October. In a summation of the fine water-colours and pen and ink drawing that show had to offer, one critic wrote:

> 'The amazing eccentricities to the perpetration of which that precocious genius Mr. Austin O. Spare, applies his rare gifts, will probably be the talk of London studios for many a day to come ... His craftsmanship is superb; his management of line has not been equalled since the days of Aubrey Beardsley; his inventive faculty is stupendous and terrifying in its creative flow of impossible horrors...'

The shy boy artist of Kennington had become the *enfant terrible* of Mayfair.

Between 1909 and 1913 Spare had several West End exhibitions whilst developing his most important work: *The Book of Pleasure*. Although he flirted briefly with Crowley during this period, it was his courtship and eventual marriage to Eiley Gertrude Shaw in 1911 that catalysed and inspired the evolution of his magical techniques. Published in 1913 *The Book of Pleasure* shows us the earlier style had given way to a finer, more subtle, pen draughtsmanship. More importantly, however, the book suggested advanced techniques for accessing what the psychologist Carl Jung would later term 'the collective unconscious' as a method of inspiring creative genius. This fundamental principle, later one of the cornerstones of Surrealism, was largely misunderstood in Edwardian London. Undeterred, in 1916 Spare founded and co-edited *Form: A Quarterly of the Arts* under the imprint of John Lane. Lavish and expensive the title folded the following year when Spare was called-up, becoming an official war artist. It was revived briefly in a modest 'second series' by Spare after the publication of his fourth book *The Focus of Life* in 1921. This latter work, a catharsis of his war experiences, delivers a dream-like narrative and visionary pencil drawings. It was

Thelemic magick I

well received, but was to be his penultimate published work. In 1924, *The Golden Hind*, of which Spare was then co-editor with Clifford Bax, ceased publication, prompting the artist to retreat to his roots in south London.

Living and working in his tiny studio in the borough Spare's anger and frustration manifested in his last published book *The Anathema of ZOS* in 1927. His exhibition at the Godfey Philips Gallery in 1930 would be the last West End show for 17 years and Spare joked with his journalist friend Hannen Swaffer that he was contemplating 'the gas oven'. However, Spare survived the Great Depression and developed a new technique for portraiture which he termed 'Siderealism'. Based on a logarithmic form of anamorphic projection it proved to be very popular success and his show of 1936 resulted in an unexpected request. Adolf Hitler received one of Spare's pastel portraits as a gift and was so impressed he asked the artist to travel to Berlin to undertake a commission. Spare refused - and became a minor celebrity! Tragically though, in 1941, at the height of the Blitz, Spare's studio in the Walworth Road received a direct hit and was completely destroyed. Spare was injured, but recovered and found a home in Brixton with an old friend Ada Millicent Pain. His exhibition at the Archer Gallery in 1947, engineered by his journalist friend Dennis Bardens, and for which he produced over 200 works, was an almost complete sell-out and ushered in his astonishing post-war renaissance.

In 1949 a youthful Kenneth Grant sought out Spare and encouraged him to return to his earlier, directly magical themes. The exhibitions and tavern shows of the early 1950s showed a mature artist of incredible vigour working at the height of his powers. At the age of sixty-eight Spare's command of the pastel medium could scarcely be equalled and he received the willing patronage of doctors, psychologists, journalists, teachers, critics and connoisseurs. His idiosyncratic modes of graphic expression, such as 'Automatism'. 'Siderealism', 'Psycho-Realism', 'Psycho-Revisionism' and 'Sigillic Formulae' remain pioneering techniques. His sudden death on May

Thelemic magick I

15th 1956, prompted many tributes mourning the loss of a singular and peculiarly English genius.

Throughout his life Spare enfleshed the Current. *The Book of Pleasure* is one of the most important magical treatises of the twentieth century, sweeping away the complex ceremony of traditional magick and introducing the simple, but infinitely powerful concepts of 'Self-Love', 'Sigils', 'The Death Posture'. His unique graphic work represents the most important corpus of magick-through-art extant. In studying one of Spare's pictures the viewer is seized by the vital energy encrypted, creating an 'en-trance' to the realms of the genius of ZOS: and thus the Current is manifest. Spare's magical systems are discussed further in the essay 'ZOS: The New Flesh of Desire' by Gavin Semple, which can be found in *Starfire* volume one number five, and will soon be appearing as a booklet under the Fulgur imprint.

Those readers interested in further information about Spare's life and work may wish to write to us via our publishing mailbox: FULGUR, BCM Fulgur, London WC1N 2XX. Details of future publications will be sent in due course. Please enclose a self-addressed stamped envelope.

Enochian Magick
By Steve Nicholls

There is an amount of scholarly dispute concerning the source material of the 'Enochian system'. Examples of disagreements include the method of numbering the Enochian alphabet and also concern different versions of the Enochian Tablets - not only John Dee's own various revisions and corrections - but also between different Golden Dawn accounts.

The Enochian magical system appeals to the intellect as well as the heart. It is one of the most powerful branches of western magick, and provides an inexhaustible area for study and practice. The potent nature of Enochian magick, with its intellectual complexity and visionary intensity, mean that it is possible to achieve effects and to progress very rapidly. It suits both individual and group work.

The *Sigillum Dei Aemeth* (The Seal of Truth) is a pure and uncoloured wax pentacle of nine inches diameter showing a complex magickal design. The Golden Dawn explains how four Sigils and four names can be derived from this Seal to channel the power of Elemental Tablets.

The Sigillum Dei Aemeth was placed under the Holy Shewstone when Kelly carried out his crystal gazing, and it works as a stabilising and enhancing influence during magickal operations rather than as a central focus for a ceremony. If placed under the table or board used for an Enochian Chess divination it should

Thelemic magick I

produce a local void within the Portal which helps to protect and intensify the game objects being worked with. No separate Opening Ritual is necessary to accompany this Seal when used with Enochian Chess after this fashion.

The *Tabula Sancta* was a wooden table, two cubits high by two cubits square which contained seven different talismans and Enochian writing in the centre and around the edge. These two items are the first two Enochian 'documents' (created in March, 1582), and the angel Uriel instructed Dee that the Seal was to be placed on the Holy Table during use.

Liber Scientia Auxilii Et Victoria Terrestris the 'Book of Science, Help and Victory', is the key to extraction of the names of 91 Angelic Princes who rule in the Thirty Aethyrs. The book also shows how the Sigils of these Princes may be drawn. The forces described in the book pertain to the world of Atziluth.

De Heptarchia Mystica contains the names, Sigils and methods of invocations for the 49 Angels of Light (of the Bonorum), and Lesser Spirits of the seven Ptolemaic planets. The Heptarchia relates to the Heavens of Assiah, and do not reach to as high a spiritual level as does the Sigillum.

The angelic entity, Nalvage, revealed *The Round Tablet Of Nalvage* which seems to have been a tool for attributing the angelic hierarchies under their proper functions. The Tablet of Nalvage contains eight rows and eight columns of letters.

The *Liber Enoch* (Liber Logeath or Log'th) details the Four Elemental Tablets (Watchtowers or Watch Towers) of Air, Fire, Water and Earth. The squares of these Tablets may contain one or more letter, either capital or lower case. The Enochian Tablets are connected by a large central cross of squares (Black Cross of the Watchtowers), the letters from which are combined to form the Tablet of Union, which represents the binding and lofty 'Element' of Spirit. A great number of important Sigils and Names can be drawn from these Tablets.

The Enochian Chess Boards consist of the Lesser Servient

Squares of the Sub-Quadrants, which are beneath (and divided by) the Names of the Angels of the Sixteen Sephirotic Crosses.

The Enochian system of John Dee is inextricably connected with his espionage work for Sir Francis Walsingham (founder of the British secret service), and his occult work on behalf of Elizabeth I.

Omphalus, Leyline, BNP house.

SOURCE: London Psychogeographical Association, 1994.[1]

Many people believe that Greenwich is the Omphalos - or spiritual centre - of the British Empire. However those with a deeper understanding of Feng Shui, the ancient Chinese art of land divination, will recognise that the actual Omphalos (naval stone) must be on the Isle of Dogs, protected by water on all sides. Those who visit the 'Mudchute' - a piece of park mysteriously built as an exact replica of an ancient hill fort - will find a special staircase leading to a cobbled circle. This is the Omphalos, the spiritual centre, where the magus John Dee conjured up the Spirit of the British Empire, in the presence of Christopher Marlowe, four hundred years ago to this year.

There is evidence to suggest that John Dee was a founder of the Rosicrucians, or at the very least a role model for them. His symbol, the Monas Hierogyphica appears in the third known Rosicrucian publication, *Die Chymische Hochzeit Christian Rosenkreutz* (published in Germany 1616, by Johann Valentin Andreae). The first Rosicrucian publication and a strong influence on the Golden Dawn tradition, was the *Fama Fraternitatus* (the Fama), published anonymously in German, 1614.

Another current idea is that Sir Francis Bacon was the founder of both Rosicrucianism and of Freemasonry. John Dee was the boyhood tutor of Francis Bacon. Both men shared an interest in ancient Egypt (via the Trismegistic literature, in Greek, since

Thelemic magick I

Egyptian writing was not then understood). Furthermore both were involved in espionage for the British Crown. Francis Bacon had introduced his old tutor to Elizabeth I, whereupon John Dee had decided the date for a propitious coronation based upon astrological considerations.

The line drawn between science and natural magick was indistinct, and both Dee and Bacon were leading proponents in both fields. It has been speculated that the 'invisible brethren' and 'invisible college' associated with the early Rosicrucians later became formalised as the Royal Society when granted a charter by Charles II.

Thomas Vaughan's translations of the *Fama* and the *Confessio* (the second Rosicrucian tract, published in Kassel, Germany, 1615) are known to have been in the library of Sir Isaac Newton. Sir Francis Bacon was a friend of Sir Thomas Bodley (founder of the Bodleian library), and sent him a copy of his first major work, *The Advancement of Learning*, 1605, which contains details of Angelic Lore, and knowledge of Persian and Egyptian magick, astrology and the planets. The 'footprints of nature' described by Bacon in his book were later illustrated in Michael Maier's 1617 Rosicrucian tract, *Atalanta fugens*. Yet another strong link between Francis Bacon and the Rosicrucian movement is his fable entitled *New Atlantis*, which clearly has parallels with the Masonic oath.

It was the writings of Bacon that inspired the first Rosicrucian community to emigrate from Europe to America. Under the leadership of Johannes Kelpius, they built a colony at Ephrata, Pennsylvania, in 1694. This group constructed the first astronomical laboratory in the western world and laid the foundations for the hugely strong Rosicrucian movement as it exists in the United States today

De Quincy, Ashmole and others have pointed to links between Rosicrucianism and Freemasonry, which reinforced suspicions on the continent that the Brotherhood had political and subversive aims, and that the professed aims of healing the sick, *gratis,* and of turning base metal into gold through alchemy were disingenuous.

Thelemic magick I

Whatever the origins of Rosicrucianism, shrouded in mystery as they are, it is apparent today that the main thrust of the movement is magickal and spiritual. Only occasionally in modern times (for instance in Aleister Crowley's accounts of his wartime collaboration with the Germans) does the notion arise that Rosicrucianism is merely a cover for the British secret service.

Robert Hooke, in addition to being a leading scientist of his day, was an expert on Cryptography. He was a keen student, even a disciple, of Dee, and took issue with critics of John Dee such as Meric Casuabon (who had written a scathing book entitled *A True and Faithful Relation of What Passed for Many Years Between Dr. John Dee and Some Spirits* in 1659). Hooke was not as gullible as many other followers of Dee, and defended Dee on grounds other than the merely superstitious interpretations that were propounded by the many flaky occultists abounding in those days (as in this).

Cryptography and secret codes seem to have their origin in the disguising of god-names. Once a god's name had been discovered, it could be used in magickal rites by the enemies of that god's people. The Romans regularly tried to discover the names of enemy gods, by bribery and espionage, in a process known by the term *elicio*. Not only was it important to discover the names of enemy gods, but it was even more vital not to have the names of your own stolen. Riddles were used often in ancient times to hide god names, as well as letter and word encryption.

In an address to the Royal Society, of which he was a member, Robert Hooke pointed out that Casaubon had missed the important point that much of Dee's writing was concerned with Cryptography, and sometimes dealt only incidentally with mysticism. With respect to Meric Casaubon's book about the *Angelic Conversations*, Robert Hooke states that:

'whatever may seem rational to others to judge of the same book, to me, I confess, it seems to be designed to comprehend another meaning than what is plainly legible in the words of it, which

Thelemic magick I

possibly many others that have read it, may have no suspicion of: neither may they have ever seen, or considered, the Cryptography of Trithemius...

The greater part of the book - especially all that which relates to the Spirits and Apparitions, together with names, speeches, prayers, etc. are all cryptography, and ... some parts also of that which seems to be a Journal of his Voyages and Travels into several parts of Germany are also cryptographic - that is, under those feigned stories, he hath concealed relations of quite another thing that he [Dee] made use of this way of absconding it that he might more securely escape discovery, if he should fall under suspicion as to the true designs of his travels, or that the name should fall into the hands of any spies as such might betray him or his intentions.

Similarly, Hooke claimed that: '*The Book of Enoch* was only for cryptographic use. . . The method was so like Trithemius that it could be transcribed by analogy thereto. There are many plain instances of cryptography.'

Hooke records in his diary for 28 April, 1677 that he: 'Saw Dee's. . . and many other books and Mss. about chymistry, conjurations, magick...' Hooke had an unusual passion for numbers and statistics, and carried out a huge amount of detective work on Dee's Enochian recordings. He also developed a game which he called 'Astrological Chess' that seem to be based, at least in part, on 'Enochian Chess'. Details are scant, but there is definite reference to 'Enochian Chess' in Hooke's writings. Whether the game goes back beyond Dee's time cannot be ascertained from the references.

The game was also used for divination and for passing messages between the two players. The 'Chess' pieces to be moved were decided by the throwing of a dice. It is a fascinating side-line of Dee's Cabbalistic equipment. . . Hooke was convinced that there two methods of playing this game: first for divination and skrying,

Thelemic magick I

sometimes in conjunction with the crystal; second, for passing messages without speaking.

In *An Ingenious Cryptographical System*, Hooke relates that:

'Mr John Marr, an excellent mathematician and geometrician and servant to King James and Charles the First, examined the precepts of the Enochian system and language as propounded and devised by John Dee and gave it as his opinion that while unquestionably this was primarily a magick system, used as such and should be interpreted as such, it also contained a most ingenious cipher or series of ciphers for conveying secret information. This system enabled a person to set out a secret message in what purported to be a confrontation between himself and spiritual creatures, or, when necessary, by the moving of objects resembling pieces of a game of chess so that each move gave an item of information. The system was further simplified in that the Enochian alphabet consisted of onlie twenty-one letters, a mightily useful economie to the cryptographer.'[2]

This passage indicates that Enochian Chess was integral and formative to the whole Enochian system of Language and Tablets, and not a Golden Dawn addition as is normally believed. The various cryptic whorls and moves which reveal the important names from the Enochian Tablets may originally have been deciphered by game pieces in the same way that the TARO magick square is deciphered by the Knight's tour.

```
S A T O R
A R E P O
T E N E T
O P E R A
R O T A S
```

Tracing over the letters using the Knight's move, we can read twice 'PATER NOSTER AO' where A and O stand for the Greek letters alpha and omega, implying the beginning and the end.

Robert Hooke develops in some detail his espionage and cryptographic theory of Enochia. What seems to be the recording of a psychedelic or magickal vision reported by Dee during June 1583, is explained by Hooke as being a coded intelligence message informing Francis Walsingham that Mary, Queen of Scots (the 'wicked Queen') had rejected her plan for launching an invasion of Scotland, and now intended to make friends with Elizabeth by associating herself with her son, James.

Hooke rejected the theory that Dee was a threadbare mystic, and points to the fact that after returning to England, supposedly destitute, he gave the Landegrave of Hesse in Germany the magnificent gift of twelve Hungarian horses - the cost of which must have been beyond even a man of moderate wealth. Furthermore, despite having had his library looted and his laboratory destroyed, John Dee was still able to pay for a new gallery in Mortlake Church.

John Dee's expeditions were as much concerned with espionage as with gathering knowledge of this and other worlds for the sake of pure learning. Many details of his relationship with Kelly might fall into place when it can be seen that the two were bonded by the higher aims and obligations of State security, rather than merely as friends who shared an interest in the occult.

Such letter puzzles based on the Knight's move (or even the moves of two different pieces alternating) were common in medieval times. Variations included Syllable, Picture and Rebus puzzles.

Magickal Squares of the Planets

By forming a grid of the number of squares of each planet, with the sum of the numbers in each column being equal, you have arrived at Magickal Squares, which are important in mathematics as well as to magick. In the magick square illustrated below the sequence of numbers in the columns and rows always adds up to 260:

Thelemic magick I

18	43	56	31	46	5	58	3
55	30	19	44	57	2	47	6
42	17	32	53	8	45	4	59
29	54	41	20	1	60	7	48
16	39	28	33	52	9	22	61
27	36	13	40	21	64	49	10
38	15	34	25	12	51	62	23
35	26	37	14	63	24	11	50

This magick square also shows a *knight's tour*, whereby the knight on an otherwise empty chessboard, visits every square on the board in turn, starting at the square numbered one above. As well as the number 260, the sum of the total of all the numbers in the square has a special significance. The method of tracing different Sigils of the planetary names from the Kameas is the Aiq Beker, or Qabalah of Nine Chambers.

The Seal or Sigil of the Planet is obtained by drawing its Kamea, and tracing a line on the square through a succession of numbers, arriving at a symmetrical design that has passed through every number. A small circle is placed on the first number to show where the name begins. The Seal is therefore an epitome or synthesis of the numbers of the Planet.

Notes
[1] Special Report 'End Masonic Mind Control'
[2] I quote directly from Richard Deacon's book *John Dee, Scientist, Geographer, Astrologer and Secret Agent* (Muller 1968) p 224 because of the importance of this passage relating to Enochian Chess.

Sound Workshop
By Jan Fries

The basic aim of last year's workshop was to discover and enjoy bizarre sounds and weird singing, i.e. the very sounds that are repressed and ignored by the speaking habits of our culture. As usual (after a long day of listening to lectures) we began by leaping around and warming up - a little motion to become aware of the living flesh. After raising some sweat, the participants were happy to rest and listen to their breath for a moment, which soon led to group howling (as we imitated wind sounds). Next came sounds such as the S, Z and SH, to imitate the sounds of water and the ocean itself, and some people found themselves swaying congruently. Then we explored vibrating the M, N and NG, the latter in rhythmic fashion (NGNGNGNG). To experience the rhythm fully all were invited to dance to express the pulsation in motions, which is a way of making rhythm easier. Vowel singing (as described in *Helrunar*[1]) was the next step. All vowels were chanted loud, medium and in a whisper and finally in the imagination and people were asked to notice their vibration and emotional response. A little earthing followed to prevent edginess and overload then we did a couple of easy rune postures for the fun of it, and earthed once more. Things got livelier when we began with 'Chaos chanting' i.e. irrational production of sound. Typical practices were the simulation of various 'shamanistic' instruments, such as rattle, drums and bass drums using the voice and dancing madly. As before, we varied the sound volume a lot so that participants found themselves dancing not only to loud chanting but also to music that took place entirely in their imagination. Indeed, ecstatic magick and shamanism do not depend on costly instruments or loud music but on associating closely with the music. This means basically that you feel the music in your body and move body to the music. As we were a bit late by

Thelemic magick I

then, the last part of the programme was fast and furious. We practiced overtone chanting in small groups and found how a number of variables (such as lip posture, mouth opening, tongue posture or motions, air pressure and the angle of the jaw) can influence a given sound. We practiced the 'L' and the 'Y' positions of the mouth and tongue and explored some of the overtones as we went along. By then the participants of the next workshop were politely banging on the door so I barely had the chance to mention Tuvinian singers, who feed their spirits using overtone chanting, and to give a hearty 'thank you' to all participants and their spirits before the next event began.

[1] *Helrunar: a manual of rune magick* by Jan Fries (Mandrake of Oxford 1993 & 2002)

The Mysteries of Lam
By Michael Staley

0. Introduction

There is a wide and growing interest in Lam stimulated by the material in Kenneth Grant's books over the last twenty years. It is impossible to talk about Lam coherently without considering the background. If Lam is an extra-terrestrial entity, then what do we mean by this term? What is the nature of such entities, and what are we in relation to them? How may we have contact with them, and to what end? In fact, I would go further, and say that the prime importance of Lam is as an example of this type. It flings the whole topic of extra-terrestrialism, and hence the heart of magick itself, into sharp relief.

At the end of this talk, it may be that not each and every one of you will go forth from this hall and immediately summon forth Lam from the recesses of your being, trafficking to your heart's content. But you will, I hope, have a clear idea of the import of the extra-terrestrial gnosis, as well as pointers as to the direction to take if you wish to move towards Lam. We will have established that to seek traffic with Lam is to seek to move beyond human consciousness.

The talk is divided into three stages. Firstly, a consideration of what we mean by the extra-terrestrial gnosis. Secondly, a consideration of the background of Lam, the seeds of which lie in the *Amalantrah Working*. Thirdly, conclusions and future directions.

1. Extra-terrestrialism

Extra-terrestrialism emerges increasingly as the core of Grant's Typhonian Trilogies. And with it an awareness that rather more is indicated than the appearance of little green men from the galaxy 10,000 million light years around the corner, or the old 'was God an astronaut?' thesis from authors such as von Daniken twenty or thirty years ago. All the same, what the extra-terrestrial gnosis means in a magickal context is not entirely unconnected, though it goes further and has a much wider, deeper and more profound sweep. Firstly, what do we mean by 'terrestrial'?

The term 'terrestrial' denotes simply that which is earth-bound, or human. The terrestrial vehicle is a mask, an incarnation of a consciousness, the veils of which dissolve in the course of initiation. 'Extra-terrestrial', therefore, indicates that which is beyond the comparatively narrow range of human, earth-bound, terrestrial consciousness. 'Beyond' or 'Outside' is often used in a similar fashion - that which lies beyond the confines of the terrestrial vehicle. What, then, is it that lies beyond these confines, and of which the terrestrial is a facet? The answer may have become a cliché, but it is potent nonetheless - cosmic consciousness.

Over recent years we have become more aware of the vast gulfs and abysses of stellar space which stretch beyond Earth, and of which Earth is a part. And there is a growing awareness of vast, unsounded reaches of consciousness, the human facet of which is a tiny portion. Extra-terrestrial entities are areas within those reaches, and the Magick of real interest and worth is that which facilitates traffic with such entities. These entities are, ultimately, not something separate from the magician: not something 'out there', but equally an aspect of the continuum of consciousness as is the magician. To explore these reaches of consciousness, traffic is had with such entities; thereby, more and more of the continuum is thrown into relief. This may seem at first sight to be a solipsist conception, the universe as nothing more than an extension of the magician. In fact, the converse is the case: the magician is an aspect of the universe, and initiation is the unfolding realisation of this, much as a temple emerges from darkness into the light of day.

A example of the use of the term 'terrestrial' in this context occurs in the first paragraph of Lovecraft's story 'Beyond the Wall of Sleep':

> From my experience, I cannot doubt but that man, when lost to terrestrial consciousness, is indeed sojourning in another and incorporeal life of far different nature from the life we know, and of which only the slightest and most indistinct memories exist after waking... We may guess that in dreams life, matter, and vitality, as the earth knows such things, are not necessarily constant; and that time and space do not exist as our waking selves comprehend them. Sometimes I believe that this less material life is our truer life, and that our vain presence on this terraqueous globe is itself the secondary or merely virtual phenomenon.

There is a continuum of consciousness, an ocean of awareness, in which we are at once parts and the whole. This is essentially *advaita*, a Sanskrit term meaning 'not divided'. Many people in the West, Thelemites included, seem to find advaita repugnant. And yet, Thelema has its roots in advaita and similar doctrines such as the *sunyavada*, the emptiness at the heart of matter, articulated so beautifully in Prajnaparamita Buddhism and later in Ch'an. Traditions such as these attempt to guide the intuition of the aspirant towards the apprehension of a non-dual reality by means of paradox. This is not indulgence in mental gymnastics, but because reality is beyond the dualist categories of subject and object, existence and non-existence, emptiness and manifestation, and hence ultimately inexpressible in terms of reason. This does not mean that we need to abandon reason, or give up trying to express mystical insight in language - far from it. We just need to be aware of the limitations of language and reason, that is all.

Magick has a mystical core - the awakening to reality, which is that there is no 'us' incarcerated in a fleshly envelope while the universe is somehow 'out there'. The emptiness at the heart of matter is simultaneously a plenitude, nourishing in its depths the potential of manifestation. Over the aeons this potential flowers in its perfection and then fades. The rhythm of the universe is maintained in a perpetual expansion and contraction, becoming and absorption. Initiation is the unveiling of consciousness; as darkness clears, more of the temple emerges into view. Initiation has been defined as 'the journey inwards', though whether this journey is viewed as an internal or external journey makes little odds, since both amount to the same thing. It is the assimilation of magickal and mystical experience - a process of understanding, of insight. The nature of this insight is an awareness that consciousness does not rest with the individual, but is universal or cosmic; there is a continuum, not a multiplicity of isolated units.

Whatever the nature of the magickal or mystical practices pursued, the real change is at the level of Jnana - intuitive knowledge. What changes is actually not consciousness, but that which we have previously thought of as ourselves in relation to it. Awareness is no longer restricted to the terrestrial vehicle; the focus shifts, attuning to wider and deeper ranges of consciousness beyond. The sense of individuality is a restriction or dungeon only so long as we incarcerate ourselves, a bondage forged by our own preconceptions. We are all facets of the universe. There is no individual self which endures, but the flux and flow of perception, like wave after wave surging forth. The wave is a transient form of the water, giving way to another wave. Consciousness roils, throwing forth shadows from its depths; these shadows are the glamours of manifestation, a perpetual play which flows and shimmers, urgent and alive, sweeping this way and that. We are drawn from these shadows: not as monads, self-existent and eternally enduring; but as transient ripples of consciousness which flow outwards, melding and coalescing with other ripples. In this incessant weaving amidst the continuum of consciousness, self and not-self mingle and fuse, slipping back and

Thelemic magick I

forth, trespassing wantonly across apparent boundaries which have always been fluid.

To become alive to this transience seems an extraordinary thing; yet it is the most natural state in the world. It is a measure of how we have cut ourselves off from reality, drawn the covers over our heads and huddled in our ghettos. Initiation is a vitriol, dissolving the illusion of separateness. Only in recognising individuality as illusion, and ceasing to cling to it, can we see past what we are not, to the fecund infinity of that which we really are. The blood is pressed into the Cup of Babalon, this continuum, this melting-pot, from whence springs the gamut of existence, and to where it returns. It is reconciliation: not of the melding of self and other, the microcosm and the macrocosm, the apparent individual and the rest of the universe, which have never been apart anyway; but of our awareness of that deeper identity.

Initiation is therefore not something which occurs to an individual. The terrestrial vehicle is a refraction of a much vaster field of awareness. As initiation runs its course, awareness becomes wider and deeper, increasingly alive to reaches which lie beyond. It is not a steady process, but unfolds by leaps of intuitive insight, a process of re-membering, of reintegration. Entities are apparent, ranges of consciousness, equally vehicles of the cosmic Self. There is a sea of sentience; we traffic with wider and deeper ranges, and there is assimilation: 'For I am divided for love's sake, for the chance of union'. Entities such as Lam and Aiwass are no more entities in their own right than are human beings: not remote, august beings, but equally shadows in the sweep of sentience.

We can see from this standpoint that there is no such thing, ultimately, as 'alien' contact. However, 'alien' has here a relative sense - wide though our assimilation of consciousness might be, until we have awoken completely then anything outside of our present conception of self is seen as 'alien'. Such is the intrusion of alien consciousness - alien, that is, to the conscious, terrestrial vehicle; alien in the sense of being beyond the self-imposed boundaries

Thelemic magick I

of that terrestrial vehicle; but ultimately not alien, since nothing exists outside consciousness. The sense of alien intrusion via the matrix of creative imagination was expressed, again by Lovecraft:

> ...The true function of fantasy is to give the imagination a ground for limitless expansion, and to satisfy aesthetically the sincere and burning curiosity and sense of awe which a sensitive minority of mankind feel towards the alluring and provocative abysses of unplumbed space and unguessed entity which press in upon the known world from unknown infinities and in unknown relationships of time, space, matter, force, dimensionality, and consciousness.[1]

Crowley's traffickings with Aiwass and Amalantrah are examples of such alien contact. Crowley usually needed a medium for such communication. In the *Amalantrah Working*, this mediumship was provided by several Scarlet Women, who were sensitised by sex, drugs, and alcohol in various exotic combinations, and became oracular. The visions experienced by the medium were frequently meaningless to her, but oracular and intended for the comprehension of Crowley. Communication was sometimes explicit; usually it was subtler, by means of numbers, symbols, I Ching hexagrams, Tarot cards, and so forth. Communication in this fashion may seem perverse and wilfully obscure. However, the use of gematria and symbols can spark intuitive leaps, flashes of insight that are not easily expressed in words. Thus, workings such as that with Amalantrah, or the *Vision and the Voice*, go beyond the subjective - although there is bound to be some such tincture, like light shining through coloured glass. These are records of alien contact, of traffic with extra-terrestrial forces, and their worth is substantiated by the fact that, years later, other occultists are able to study these records and make creative use of them, continuing with some of the threads.

For the magician, the first clear instance in his or her initiation of sustained, extra-terrestrial contact is characterised as the Knowledge and Conversation of the Holy Guardian Angel - a contact regarded as bestowing occult puberty. The Angel is of a nature which is beyond the terrestrial vehicle, and of which the mind can retain only fleeting glimpses. Again, the Angel is no passive entity: on the contrary, the initial impulse for the Knowledge and Conversation comes from the Angel, not the aspirant.

It is with this continuum of consciousness, this matrix, that we traffic when making 'alien' contact. As we become increasingly alive to those vast reaches of consciousness which lie beyond the terrestrial, so there grows a corresponding awareness that we are not confined to the terrestrial vehicle through which we have habitually focussed. There is a sensation of recognition, of remembrance, of experiencing again an intrinsic state which had slipped awhile beyond conscious recall. This state remains as a substratum, the hidden stream or current which powers the fountain. The Holy Guardian Angel dwells at this point, where the terrestrial merges into the infinite and eternal; it is the point which is everywhere and at all times, veiled by the chimera of identity with the terrestrial vehicle, revealed by the dissolution of that chimera. The Angel is ever present, a fountain of living waters from which we can drink at any time. Magickal and mystical experience is the life-blood of initiation, a stream from which we are eternally supping.

Against this background of the extra-terrestrial continuum of consciousness, the nature of entities and the unfolding of initiation, let us now move on to focus more specifically on Lam.

2. Origins of Lam

Crowley's portrait of Lam, entitled 'the Way', was first published in 1919 as a frontispiece to his Commentary on Madame Blavatsky's *The Voice of the Silence*. Blavatsky's text is about the need for the aspirant to contact the well-spring within, the mystical core of being, which she epitomised as the voice of the silence. The techniques which she advocates for this are meditational. It is, I think, significant that Crowley associated the portrait with this text, indicating quite clearly that he regarded Lam as the embodiment of that voice.

Thelemic magick I

Other than this, nowhere in Crowley's work is there a mention of the portrait of Lam until 1945, when he recorded in his diary Kenneth Grant's interest in it. It is clear, however, that the portrait arose in connection with the *Amalantrah Working* of 1918-19, when Crowley lived in New York. Unfortunately, the record of that working which survives consists of the first six months only. Nevertheless, it is clear from a study of this surviving material that the portrait of Lam embodies the quintessence of the working.

The absence of Crowley's exegesis on Lam gives us a great deal of freedom and creativity to discover the implications for ourselves, and to use them as magickal and mystical tools in our initiation. The portrait was republished in Grant's book *The Magical Revival* in 1972, and several times since. There is much material on Lam in the more recent books by Grant; however, a definitive interpretation has yet to develop. This is because we are dealing with something the import of which is only just emerging.

A broad outline has become apparent, though, sufficient to emphasise the primary function of Lam as the gateway to wider and deeper ranges of consciousness - our extra-terrestrial, pan-dimensional reality. In fact, anything whatsoever can function as the gateway to those dimensions. The supreme glyph of enlightenment is the lightning-flash, the swift awakening to reality, which illuminates the landscape previously shrouded in darkness. The lightning flash can be triggered at any time, and by anything, when the conditions are propitious. The accumulation of glamour around the cult of Lam makes it a gateway which is pre-eminently accessible, however.

As the *Voice of the Silence*, Lam is the Babe-in-the-Egg, Harpocrates, the God-of-Silence. The association is underlined by the assignation of 71 to both the portrait and the Commentary, as is made clear by the inscription which accompanied the portrait as originally published:

Lam is the Tibetan word for way or path, and Lama is 'he who goeth', the specific title of the Gods of Egypt, the Treader-of-the-Path, in Buddhistic phraseology. Its numerical value is 71, the number of this book.

A metathesis of LAM is ALM, also 71, a Hebrew word meaning 'silence, silent'. The silence is the noumenon which underlies and infuses phenomena, the continuum of which all things whatsoever are simultaneously facets and the whole. The silence is the quietness at the heart of noise, the stillness at the heart of activity, the being at the heart of going, and the emptiness at the heart of matter. These juxtapositions may seem merely revelling in paradox; the fact is, though, that reason is a tool of limited application, and paradox is a means of pointing beyond apparent contraries. The 'way' or 'path' is a reference to the Tao. The 'Treader of the Path' is the Initiate, treading the path of initiation. This brings to mind the concluding lines from 'Pilgrim-Talk', in Crowley's the *Book of Lies*:

> O thou that drawest toward the End of The Path, effort is no more. Faster and faster dost thou fall; thy weariness is changed into Ineffable Rest.

> For there is no Thou upon That Path: thou hast become The Way.

Harpocrates or Hoor-paar-kraat is the unmanifest twin of Ra-Hoor-Khuit, manifestation. The distinction between these twins is figurative only; they are aspects of each other, neither separate from the other. The term 'Dwarf-Self' is often used: of yet to manifest, adolescent, prepubescent. This is the Hidden God, a term used throughout the *Egyptian Book of the Dead* to glyph the sun in the Underworld or Amenta, the radiant heart of dynamic energy which is at the core of manifestation, and which is veiled by the image of Shaitan-Aiwaz, 93. Hoor-paar-kraat is a term often used synonymously with the Holy Guardian Angel. It may also be seen in terms of the Tetragrammaton, where Ra-Hoor-Khuit is the Vau, and Hoor-paar-kraat the He, final. This identifies Hoor-paar-kraat with the Aeon of Maat, the continuum or extra-terrestrial reality, a communion in which we are at once celebrants and that which is celebrated. As Treaders of the Way, we are not something separate

Thelemic magick I

which merely traverses from one point to another: we are the way.

Crowley went to the United States in 1914, at the outbreak of the First World War, and stayed there until 1919. This period covers the core of his initiation into the A∴A∴ grade of Magus. They were years marked by an ever- deepening insight into and affinity with Taoism, as is made plain in the course of the Preface to his version of the *Tao Teh Ching*. This insight saturates *Liber Aleph, The Book of Wisdom or Folly*, the manuscript of which was almost complete by the opening of the *Amalantrah Working*. *Liber Aleph* is a central work of Crowley's, where he makes clear the deep affinity between Taoism and Thelema; without an appreciation of this affinity, *Liber Aleph* appears as little more than a scattering of aphorisms. The *Amalantrah Working* needs to be seen in the context of this initiation of Crowley's.

According to Crowley's account, the working arose spontaneously. He was living with a mistress at the time, Roddie Minor. One of her indulgences was opium, the opulent visions of which she related aloud. On one particular occasion, her apparent ramblings struck Crowley as bearing on the *Abuldiz Working* of some years previously, and after some astral investigation he decided that there were indeed threads of the earlier working which were being picked up; thus opened the *Amalantrah Working*. Crowley inaugurated regular sessions, which usually took place at the weekends. He seemed interested primarily in its use as an oracle for his affairs over the forthcoming week. Although there were many such short- term oracular pronouncements, there was also a wealth of more substantial material.

Amalantrah is the name of the entity with whom Crowley trafficked over the course of the working. Communication was never direct, but via a medium or Seer who was sensitised by sex, drugs and alcohol in various combinations. Because of the effects of these preliminaries, the earthing of the communications was often poor, their expression rambling and diffuse; the wheat needs to be separated from the chaff, therefore, when considering the Record.

Thelemic magick I

The seer was usually Roddie Minor, although on a few occasions other women did assume the office. The visions often opened in a woodland temple which was perceived astrally by the seer; this temple was sometimes peopled by doubles of those participating, and as well as on occasion absent colleagues.

The name 'Lam' never occurs in the surviving record of the *Amalantrah Working*. It is, though, the root of several of the names which do occur. The portrait of Lam is in fact a composite glyph embodying the essence of the working. Several of the early visions are very suggestive of the portrait of Lam. Consider, for example, the following:

> I began by asking for a vision containing a message. I first heard gurgling water and saw a dark farmhouse in among trees and green fields. The house and other things disappeared, and a dark yoni appeared just where the house had stood. I then asked 'where will a message come from?' Immediately, soldiers with guns appeared lounging about the place, and a king on a throne where the house had stood. I then asked again for a message, and saw an egg in which were many tiny convolutions of some flesh-like substance which would form something. The egg was placed in an oblong as in a picture. Around it were clouds, trees, mountains and water, called the 'four elements'. A camel appeared in front of the whole picture. I next tried to find out who the king was. He looked more like Professor Shotwell than any one else. That is, he was 'simple, democratic' and very learned and fine. He was certainly not a king belonging to any kingdom limited by a country's borders, but he was a king of men, or a king of the world. I asked his name and the word 'Ham' appeared between the egg in the oblong and the soldiers around the king.

The egg is a commonly-occurring glyph throughout the visions of the *Amalantrah Working*. It is of course a glyph of birth - the egg which contains the potential of all that is to come. There is a reference in one of the visions to Geburah 'applied to' the egg.

Thelemic magick I

Geburah is in this context the sword which cleaves the egg, or the lightning flash which sunders it, giving birth to the potential secreted within. Since elements of this particular vision are the foundation for much of the subsequent analysis, an extract from the record follows. Roddie Minor, the seer, whose magickal name is Achitha, is questioned by Crowley:

> A: 'Wizard very serious and looks at Achitha in a very contemplative mood. Seems to approve. Turtle is most prominent thing in Temple. Child is there, lion and Barzedon. Arcteon has a very prominent place; he is a tall man that always appears in the Temple.'
>
> T: 'What is the work of this weekend?'
>
> A: 'Geburah.'
>
> T: 'Geburah applied to what?'
>
> A: 'The egg. The egg is resting on the point of mountain tops, very sharp. Water around, lotus flowers on it.'
>
> T: 'Egg is symbol of some new knowledge, isn't it?'
>
> A: 'Gimel. Lamed.'
>
> T: 'What does that mean?'
>
> A: 'I don't know; followed symbol of mountain and lotus flower.'
>
> T: 'How are we to break open the egg?'

Thelemic magick I

A: 'In plain language it means: Thou art to go this Way.'

T: 'That isn't plain language. How are we to get this new knowledge?'

A: 'Don't ask questions too fast. Sow the wild oats; go into the... into the Mother... to be born again.'

T: 'What about the Mass of the Holy Ghost?'

A: 'That hasn't anything to do with it. You've shattered everything. I'll have to establish connection all over again... Going into the Mother to be born again, you get a New Life and then the Earth is covered with wonderful flowers, and bees come to the flowers to get honey to store, and the honey is stored elixir. I see a hill very steep. Mother standing... down... watching child. I don't know if she's going to save it, or go after it, or what. Lotus flower on water again.'

The references to the lotus flower in association with the egg, and later the child, are significant. They suggest the Babe in the Egg, Harpocrates, often depicted as seated upon a lotus flower. The mountain is a symbol of initiation, of communing with the gods; examples are Mount Arunachala and Mount Kailash and the story of Moses ascending the mountain to receive the word of God.

The Hebrew letters Gimel and Lamed give GL, which means 'spring, fountain'. The portrait of Lam clearly shows a mottled emanation or umbra from the top of the egg. This is like the dappled effect of a fountain in sunlight. More to the point, though, it clearly glyphs the fountain of dew which showers from the Sahasrara chakra when the Fire Snake streaks up the Sushumna. This is especially interesting, because Lam is the bija-mantra of the Muladhara Chakra, which is the home of the Fire Snake. We have here something more forceful than the more common conception of

Thelemic magick I

silence and being. There is a perichoresis, or interpenetration of dimensions between the aspirant, the Fire Snake, and the manifested universe. The Shakti which manifests as the universe, and the Shakti which is concentrated as the Fire Snake, are not two: they are the same. In *Outer Gateways*, Grant speaks of 'the dynamic energies of consciousness, the functions of which are to blast away the delusion of separate existence'.

The portrait of Lam also shows a well-developed Ajna chakra, which can be seen as a stylised ankh. Together with the pattern of the umbra mentioned earlier, the shape of a cup or chalice is clearly there. GL also means a 'bowl' or 'chalice'. In the record of the last surviving session of the Amalantrah Working, Gimel and Lamed are mentioned as being the two sides of perfection. This suggests that if Gimel and Lamed are the two sides of perfection, and Gimel and Lamed as the bowl or chalice, then perfection is the supreme chalice or Graal, the Cup-of-Babalon, the womb of the mother. This interpretation is underlined by a passage in Crowley's commentary to *Liber LXV (The Book of the Heart Girt with the Serpent)*:

> P, is the letter of Atu XVI the 'House of God' or 'Blasted Tower'. The hieroglyph represents a Tower - symbolic of the ego in its phallic aspect, yet shut up, i.e. separate. This Tower is smitten by the Lightning Flash of Illumination, the impact of the H.G.A. and the Flaming Sword of the Energy that proceeds from Kether to Malkuth. Thence are cast forth two figures representing by their attitude the letter Ayin: these are the twins (Horus and Harpocrates) born at the breaking open of the Womb of the Mother (the second aspect of the Tower as 'a spring shut up, a fountain sealed').

This passage underlines the mention earlier of Geburah 'applied to' the egg, the lightning flash being in this context a type of Geburah. Perfection also suggests the Tao. Crowley assigned the number 157 to his edition of the *Tao Teh Ching*. This is the addition of 83 and 74, the values of Gimel and Lamed spelt in full, thus

Thelemic magick I

reinforcing the reference to them as the two sides of perfection. We have, then, an identity between the Tao and the Cup of Babalon, both being perfection; and, of course, 'the Perfect and the Perfect are one Perfect and not two; nay, are none!' (AL.I.45). The reference to 'a spring shut up, a fountain sealed' is from the *Song of Solomon*:

> A garden barred is my sister, my bride, a spring shut up, a fountain sealed.

This indicates a pregnant womb, rather than a celebration of virginity: to shut up or seal is to obstruct something which has formerly flowed. In the womb is the hermit, Hoor-paar-kraat, the 'secret seed', the Hidden God, released from the egg by the shattering force of the lightning flash of illumination. In *Olla*, Crowley defines Silence as the Path of the Lightning Flash. Silence in this context is not simply the absence of noise or movement: it is the 'still, small voice', Hadit or the Bindu from which manifestation unfolds, the potential which gives rise to the actual, the noumenon which underlies phenomena. The Egg of Silence is typified by Lam; to embark on the Cult of Lam is therefore to evoke the Hidden God, the Holy Guardian Angel. This is initiation, the journey inwards which is simultaneously the journey outwards, for the microcosm and the macrocosm are not two but one.

This gateway, and these trances, are nothing new. The goal of all magickal and mystical traditions is gnosis - the awakening to reality. The nominalisations of this goal are legion, but all paths lead to Rome. Similarly, each Initiate will have his or her own gateway, but each gateway will open out onto the same reality. In the course of my own magickal work, I have developed the following short invocation of the gateway:

> Lam! Thou Voice of the Silence, Glyph of Hoor-paar-kraat: The Dwarf-Self, the Hidden God. Gateway to the Aeon of Maat! I evoke Thee! I evoke Thee! With the mantra Talam-Malat,

Thelemic magick I

Talam-Malat, Talam-Malat.....

This evocation concentrates some of the themes which we have touched upon. The mantra 'Talam-Malat' celebrates the Lam as the gateway, and is uttered several times before it lapses into silent vibration. 'Talam' is the semen-honey offered in the Mass of Maat; the word is a fusion of Lam and Maat. Its number is 81, KSA, the full moon which is both the flowering of the lunar cycle and the point of return to the New Moon; similarly, Maat is both the flowering of the Aeonic cycle and the point of return to the *pralaya* or dissolution. The second half of the mantra, 'Malat', a mirror image of the first half, emphasises this sense of backward-turning.

The use of this mantra stems from the culminating moon of a working, based on Crowley's *Liber Samekh*, which I undertook several years ago after sensing a summons to the Knowledge and Conversation of the Holy Guardian Angel. The number 81 emerged into awareness, and it seemed to be a fusion of several elements - my growing interest in Lam, the mysteries of Maat into which I was then gaining an insight, and my Angel. The mantra 'Talam-Malat', then, concentrates and celebrates the common nature and indeed identity of the Angel, the Aeon of Maat, the Tao, and extra-terrestrialism. This insight was, and is, a matter of experience; once tasted, the nectar is not only never forgotten, but is ever-present.

This brings us back to the prime consideration of the Cult of Lam, which is that though Lam is the gateway to our extra-terrestrial reality, that gateway is intrinsic to the individual Initiate. Similarly, the key that unlocks the gateway is necessarily of a unique pattern, and must be discovered by the Initiate in the course of direct magickal and mystical experience. The cult of Lam focuses upon the techniques for discovering the pattern. However, these techniques can never be a universal template; rather, they are but a basis upon which the Initiate rears his or her own temple of illumination, the inner shrine of which is silence.

3. Future Directions

Having heard these considerations about the nature of extra-terrestrial entities, alien contact, and the continuum from which they all spring; having heard a preliminary analysis of the meaning and import of Lam from the *Amalantrah Working*, where do we go from here?

It is my own view that, in the light of the ground which we have covered in this talk, Lam is analogous to the Holy Guardian Angel. Thus, to embark upon trafficking with Lam is to seek the Knowledge and Conversation. Now, there is no one technique to seek the Knowledge and Conversation. There are things like *Liber Samekh*, *The Sacred Magic of Abramelin*, and so forth. However, the point about the Angel is that it is not the aspirant who calls forth the Angel, but the Angel who calls forth the aspirant. In the absence of the impulse from the Angel, even *Liber Samekh* will be sterile. The Angel is not some entity with a message in a bottle for the aspirant, but a much greater, pan-dimensional being of whom the aspirant is just a facet. Lam is then a Gateway to Initiation; one amongst many, true, but the glamour around the Cult of Lam makes it an accessible Gateway.

In my own magickal work, a being with an egg-shaped head has not appeared to me. But then I never expected that. My work upon Lam has been largely of a contemplative nature. For instance, I use a simple ceremony, opening with the Lesser Banishing Pentagram, and moving onto the Lesser Invoking Hexagram, utilising the Hexagram of Earth. I then utter the evocation read out a few minutes ago, allowing the mantra to lapse into silence, and follow it. This may seem unspectacular, but I have always regarded magick as being work on consciousness, of widening and deepening awareness. Magick has a mystical core, without which it holds no interest.

All the same, I am interested in developing techniques that are of use to the aspirant in finding his own unique way to and through Lam. In pursuance of this, I will soon be embarking on group working with several colleagues, focusing around joint visualisation,

Thelemic magick I

concentration and the reverberation of mantra. If this approach proves fruitful, the results and any developments of those results will be disseminated in *Starfire* and elsewhere. Similarly, if any other individuals or groups have techniques which they would care to share, we would all be very interested.

Anyway, I hope that I have demonstrated in the course of this talk that there is a background of which Lam is a type, and have in the course of it shed some light on the nature of Lam. The Cult of Lam is in its infancy - it is, after all, the Babe in the Egg - and I am sure that it has the potential to develop into an extremely potent Gateway to Initiation.

Notes

[1] The reference to these 'alluring and provocative abysses' pressing in, is not to something passive and quiescent, scenery to be admired, but something to reach out for and actively make themselves felt.

Cut Up and Collage in Magick
By Dave Lee

I've been making collages from newscuttings and magazine pictures for some years. What started out as an amusement I came to realise was a fascinating and powerful magickal tool. The first collage I made was made for fun - it was a kind of advert for Chaos Magick. It incorporated - for reasons I don't remember or never made conscious - a newsclipping of Jim and Tammy Bakker, the American evangelists, with the words 'pleased about buggings' around them. The week that I first photocopied the collage it was announced on the news that they had been caught up in some corruption scandal. This was my first hint that collage could be a magickal method, even when not consciously applied for magickal results.

A couple of years later, I completed another collage. This contained some fairly emotionally-charged material for me, derived from articles about religion, particularly catholicism, including a large image of the Pope. The day that I showed it to someone else for the first time, it was announced that the Pope had cancer. Looking back at the collage, I saw that I had surrounded the picture of the Pope with the phrases 'Gene Fun', 'Courting Chaos', and 'they're muties, Quint'. On further examination, there were more connecting themes in the collage, none of which were placed there with any specific magickal intent. The juxtapositions happened,

Thelemic magick I

without my conscious mind knowing why at the time.

After this, I began to experiment with deliberate collage magick. The next one I made was part of a magickal working involving a number of other people, and we got a positive result. However, it could have been the other work that was done that connected with the result. I had a feeling that the collage in itself would have failed, for the following reason: it was too deliberate and serious, too heavy-handed, compared with the lightness of touch of the earlier ones. So, I began to attempt to recapture that lightness. I found the use of advertising slogans helpful, and headlines from tabloid newspapers, because of their incredible superficiality.

An analogous technique is the use of scrapbooks. Many years ago, a magickal acquaintance of mine was experimenting with the construction of scrapbooks of pictures which he wanted to be in. His scrapbooks were kept like photograph albums, like a record of a life he had already lived. He achieved a number of positive results with this simple method.

An extension of the collage technique is to use song lyrics as triggers for enchantments. A colleague of mine has developed this into a highly effective sorcery technique. It involves choosing a line from a pop song which represents her intent, then hiding the intention by typing out another line from the same song. This line is introduced into letters and collages which are sent to other people. If the recipient knows the song lyrics, the song will start playing in his head, including the key line. There are other levels of subtlety to this procedure which can be added according to the ingenuity of the operator.

Moving on to sound cut-up, I shall let the master himself introduce the techniques. William S Burroughs has released an album called *Breakthrough in Grey Room*, which contains examples of numerous styles of audio cut-up. Without the benefit on the page of playing these samples, I shall give a brief list:

1. The intercutting ('drop-in technique') of two voices. In this instance, Burroughs and his lover Ian Sommerville make the tape

Thelemic magick I

together. This is an example of the kind of cut-up that can be used to forge a bond between two people, such as a love spell (if you are unwise enough to perform such an inevitably disastrous operation!).

2. Present time exercise: Burroughs reads out a spontaneous description of what he is experiencing at that moment. This tape is then an island in time, which forms the basis for: a) time travel experiments, evoking precise nostalgias of time and place and b) 'dislocation in time' enchantments. In this technique, recordings are made of the target place, then further recordings are made at later dates. Intercutting the different recodings produces a sense of dislocation in time, which Burroughs claims to have used in various successful curses.

An example of how such a tape might be used is given in Burroughs's novel *Cities of the Red Night*. Clem Snide the Private Asshole is investigating the disappearance of a boy. He goes to the boy's last apartment, and, whilst spinning the tape randomly back and forth, records ambient sounds - doors shutting, taps, toilet flushing and so on. He thereby creates a sound-picture of the boy's environment. He takes this home and uses it as a background to an act of sex magick aimed to find the boy.

3. Breaking words down into chaotic sound: the repeated use of cut-up and overlay on a tape, or the use of a reel-to-reel machine to 'inch' the tape back and forth across the heads, can produce a complete destruction of the original words. The words are triturated out of existence. Sounds like animal voices, machine noises and so on can result. In my experience, high levels of distortion can produce a similar kind of alienness and destruction of subjectivity. Such tapes can be used for attaining bizarre gnoses for deep-trance work.

A variant of these techniques is to employ a fast channel-changer on a TV to produce a random picture for divination. I was staying with a friend who had a remote control that would cycle rapidly through the channels whilst the screen remained blank. I focused on

Thelemic magick I

my question, then hit the 'stop' button. The resultant TV sequence proved to be a perfect answer to my question.

The power of cut-ups and collages is a subtle, personal art that must be experienced to be appreciated. Try it!

BABALON
By M C Medusa

A shortened version of this talk was delivered to the participants at the Babalon ritual. It was later presented to the January 1995 meeting of the Golden Dawn Occult Society under the title: *Tasting The Grail And Other Ecstasies*.

This article is drawn from the fruits of several years magickal work with BABALON.* As such it largely incorporates material from those workings, their aftermath and various meditations. It also includes ideas drawn from a few other people's writings. The article explores who Babalon is, working with Babalon and a couple of other issues besides.

BABALON as a New Aeon Deity

Babalon as a deity is entirely Thelemic, i.e. she has no history or mythology outside that current. This is both confusing and exciting. We tend to lend more credence to that which we can research from the work of others and rely on this as a means of verifying our own

---

* Editor's Note: It is normal for magicians to render god names in block capitals to draw attention to special qualities of the name itself. The spelling BABALON was corrected or 'restored' to its original Qabalistic spelling by Crowley. For ease of reading, it will be retyped as Babalon throughout the rest of this article.

Thelemic magick I

ideas. However, there is to my knowledge, little in the way of written material on Babalon.

Crowley's writings on her are scattered and limited. In the section on Babalon in *Magick* he states that such matters are too sacred to be printed and are only to be communicated by him to 'chosen pupils' in private instruction. (Spot the ulterior motive?!) He does refer to her in other places and in my opinion, his essay on Atu XI, Lust, in the *Book of Thoth* is much more revealing. Jack Parsons worked with Babalon extensively and his *Book of Babalon* is well worth reading. I have come across nothing written on Babalon by women working with either of these magicians which strikes me as odd not to mention frustrating. Maybe the women concerned did not write anything, or did not want it published or else someone somewhere is holding it back. In more recent times, Linda Falorio is the only person I have come across who has published anything.

Parsons discusses one aspect of Babalon as being a necessary counterbalance to Horus, the god of the New Aeon. According to him, Horus represents a blind force or violent energy dependent on those who channel it for definition. Babalon provides Love, understanding and Dionysian freedom to counteract the possible overweening control of Horus. In this Babalon provides the crucial understanding of our own natures (i.e. the beast), the disguised lusts and fears. It is the energy of Horus that breaks down old institutions and ideas, it is Babalon who ensures that understanding develops from this and that one institution is not simply replaced by another.

But all this amounts to little and thus the lack of history and mythology on Babalon becomes exciting. We are thrown back upon ourselves, upon our own experience of the deity. It seems the only way we can gain knowledge of her is by opening ourselves up to her and allowing her to reveal to us the knowledge and experience which we seek. As such we as practising magicians create the myth of Babalon, perhaps more so than with other deities whose myths and legends are well documented and easily accessible.

Thelemic magick I

The Babylon that is railed against in the *New Testament* is glorified in the New Aeon as Babalon and Mary, as Crowley says, is blasphemy, she shuts herself up, and in the New Aeon, the word of sin is restriction. In the form of Babalon, redemption stands on its Tantrik head, it's all down to you! Coming to know Babalon is no armchair experience, she is demanding of your undivided attention, so on with the Act.

Working with Babalon

The image of 'Babalon' is for me very much the image portrayed in the tarot card from the Thoth deck (Lust XI). Having encountered the image some time before I began any ritual working with her it seemed entirely appropriate and certainly a potent image of the energy encapsulated by this deity. I have not found it necessary to use another image of my own making, although I have encountered images in my own visions. The image in the Thoth deck seems to me a complete glyph and is striking enough to feed the deeper reaches of being and be readily usable.

It is easy to get a general feel for the type of energy that Babalon encapsulates from this image. The heads of the beast might be seen as representative of the types of qualities expressed by her. Alternatively, or even simultaneously, the heads might be seen as representative of the life force and inspired living that Babalon so demands. Your own meditations on this will lead you to your own ideas. She rides the beast indicating their union and holds the reins representative of the Will to unite, a cup is held aloft in ecstatic gnostic gesture. Babalon rides the beast as a result of the Will to unite and as such expresses Love under Will.

This indicates that riding the beast is being at one with the beast rather than riding the beast in an attempt to exert control over it. Control comes as a result of the union; 'for pure will unassuaged of purpose is in every way perfect.' Attempting to exert control over the beast, say by acts of repression, merely feeds the demons who wish to keep the bestial power for themselves rather than seeing you

Thelemic magick I

liberated in cosmic union and themselves redundant! In order to attain this union, it is necessary to surrender *everything* to Babalon. It is the price we pay for magickal knowledge and power, in this respect we encounter Babalon in every act of magick if it is done correctly and Babalon as a deity enshrines an essential magickal principle. I find it useful to think of Babalon in this context as taking everything I offer one stage further than my capacity at that time allows, thus ensuring I hold nothing back and all is given either unto her or certainly unto the magickal act which at this point becomes the same thing.

Babalon demands of her devotees every drop of ecstasy. Her magick incorporates a very physical sensation, as well as a magickal one. Working with Babalon makes us aware of the body as something that actually is life, rather than a vehicle whose purpose is to get you through it. The body is thus the perfect vehicle for this expression of ecstasy which is taken here in a broad sense. Babalon is a deity of extremes of passion; as such she demands all extremes of experience, all pain, sorrow, suffering, joy, love, beauty, sadness, blood, sweat, tears and laughter all belong to her. Surrendering yourself to these extremes of emotion can give release to huge amounts of physical energy resulting in orgasm, which according to some schools of thought is crucial to our well being. Orgasms attained ritually or by other means, is surprisingly enough, also sacred to Our Lady Babalon! The cup is particularly significant in this context. It is taken to represent Understanding as the wand is taken to represent Will. It is the vessel into which we place everything and consequently lose our identity in that moment of ecstatic gnosticism.

Deny *nothing*. Give joyously on the birth of creation, give with abandon and receive all Love. Babalon, lady of the wild beasts, sister of Pan embracing lusty ecstatic nature.

Refuse this giving, deceive yourself to believe it is your secret to harbour, and know the thrashing sword, for she will come and take, wrench all from those who do not give freely of their Love to

Babalon; thus they are destroyed. Those who give must live knowing the secret of Eternity for they have drunk to the Holy Whore and have tasted the wine of the Grail.

Such are the demands Babalon makes. My own visions of her are of vibrant beauty, powerful physical essence, vigour and strength. It is a dancing changing movement of potent sexuality and as such might be similar to the Eastern concept of Shakti. However, the energy has a sense of direction. An analogy that strikes me is that of the fieriness of molten lava at the core of the earth which can be directed to a final form and repeatedly cast back into the fire to be reformed as we (re)form our Will. There is an alchemical link here indicated in the offering of all to Babalon for transmutation.

Babalon and Tantra.

There is most certainly a link here. Working with Babalon provided a useful link for me to begin working with Tantrik material and concepts. Within Tantra there is a precept of Will known as *Svecchachara* meaning following the path of your own true will, it is also central to Thelema and consequently to Babalon as a major Thelemic energy. It is also known that Crowley spent time in the East studying yoga magick and it is highly likely that the ideas and practices he encountered there filtered through into his work with Thelema.

In the Thoth deck image, Babalon can be seen trampling the bodies of the dead saints whose blood she carries in her cup. I have also had visions of her trampling on the bodies of those who breathe but do not live, of those who do not offer their all to Babalon and as such deny their life. In this aspect she appears similar to Kali who will sever your head out of love for you and thus bring liberation.

Babalon will take you on a journey of carnal delights. As such she encompasses a Tantrik fervour, the strong sexual imagery and the trampling of dead souls can also be seen in the context of breaking taboos, both social and personal, and as daring to Love. These elements are represented strongly in Tantra as a means to liberation.

Thelemic magick I

It is the ridding of unnecessary elements no longer useful to the fulfilment of our Will while the sexual act represents ourselves in liberated expression. Crowley writing on Babalon had an awareness of this when he says:

> ... for to each individual thing attainment means first and foremost the destruction of the individuality.

These things challenge the very fabric of your universe. Babalon is demanding. As I said earlier, this is no armchair experience.

Babalon and the Scarlet Woman

This area seems to be a hot-bed of confusing issues. The two names are virtually synonymous. Scarlet Woman was used by Crowley and Parsons to describe avatars of Babalon, who of course would be women (or a particular woman in the case of Parsons). Women generally were also seen by Parsons as partaking of the nature of Babalon in the New Aeon which he saw manifest in the growing women's consciousness at the time and the rise in lesbianism and female polygamy. Whether there was an actual rise or whether it just became more known about is irrelevant.

On the issue of gender, I am not of the opinion that Babalon is exclusive to female energy though this might traditionally be so even in Thelema. Any difficulties encountered by magicians working with deities of the opposite gender to the one they dominantly express is usually a reflection of their own inhibitions and imaginations rather than any inherent biological limitations. In fact, it might be that exploring different gender forms is entirely appropriate to Babalon if we consider the previously mentioned issues of taboo breaking which are pertinent to her. It seems to me that the stereotyped female experience of magick as an expression of sexuality, devotion and passivity (i.e. the ability to surrender) is as limiting to men as it is to women, sexual preferences aside. This is particularly true of passivity, which in terms of surrender might be equated with giving

Thelemic magick I

oneself up in the sexual act to your lover, or as in this case, to Babalon.

Passivity in Hindu tantrism has different gender associations; Shakti is active and Shiva is the passive aspect of will. In Buddhist tantrism this relationship is reversed, Shakti is passive wisdom and the Boddhisattva the active principle. Passivity and activity are mutually reliant concepts. There can be neither one without the other. In this respect, I tend to think that they express an immediate dualism on which dynamic the universe and ourselves are created. As such both aspects exist in each of us and are not gender specific. I imagine this dynamic to be what has driven sacred ritual through time immemorial.

So where does this notion of passivity come from and why is it viewed as the exclusive domain of women and somehow therefore not as good, weaker and less important than activity? I have to say, I don't know, and neither does anyone else as far as I can make out. There is no particularly good evidence that at one time women were completely honoured (or even ruled) and then one day men got the upper hand, redefined and devalued feminine concepts and it's been that way since.

I do think that there is quite clearly an emphasis on these ideas about women throughout the industrialisation of the western world. However magically there are no excuses for holding these notions and to be honest, I don't actually know any male magicians who do, or at least are prepared to admit publicly that they do.

Crowley might have something to answer for here, as a still widely read magician and still a significant force in many people's magickal career. His attitudes to women have often been cited, but one more time eh? At best he appears confused and at worst bigoted and hypocritical. On the one hand he suggests that if you (presumably male) find that she (presumably your scarlet woman, irrespective of whether or not she knows this) should find that she will not comply with your wishes, then a few compliments will soon render her at your mercy. He is talking here of using orgasm to develop an astral

Thelemic magick I

body but this is probably only one of many examples. On the other hand, it is easy to see how Crowley was in awe of, and adored, the feminine principle as his invocations to Babalon and Nuit attest. He also talks of how women of the New Aeon will be 'girt with sword' etc., and this is certainly my impression of most women I meet today, irrespective of whether or not they practice magick. They would quite happily wield their swords at the balls of any man coming out with such crap.

The idea that only women can channel feminine energy is also a hangover from feminism. What was at one point quite a radical idea as women began to explore their psyches with attitude has been retained in some feminist popular press on New Agey type magic. As I said, I don't uphold this idea, but do support aspects of feminism as women are still discriminated against in society.

Babalon I feel does however have an important place for women practising magick today as she truly elevates the feminine principle into a wilful, dynamic life force, which Crowley among others, seems to be aware of, but does not apparently live out. This activity, the act that Babalon demands, is I think how women on the magickal scene can raise their profile rather than bemoaning how sexist the scene is, or how inaccessible Crowley is to female magicians.

Finally, Babalon encompasses the Scarlet Woman as she encompasses other derogatory old Aeon phrases such as Whore, and raises them aloft as they express both qualities with which she likes to be invoked and a certain freedom (that scarlet women and whores have historically been famous for) which she imparts upon being invoked.

My joy is the joy of eternity, and my laughter is the drunken laughter of a harlot in the house of ecstasy. (Parsons)

Reading
Aleister Crowley, *Liber ABA: Book Four-Magick* (Weiser 1995)
The Book of Thoth (Weiser)

Thelemic magick I
Magick Without Tears (Llewellyn)
Linda Falorio, *Kiss The sky!* (xerox)
Linda Falorio, *Voices of Babalon* (Headless Press)
Jack Parsons, *Freedom is a Two Edged Sword* (Falcon Press)

Wild Mandrakes
History of Fun
Mary Hedger

ISBN 1869928636 £8.99 in paper
In an explicit sex magick orgy, History of Fun recounts the origins of a powerful occult phenomenon, the cult of Thelema. Artist and mother Est, can no longer numb the magnetic pull of her destiny with drugs. Newly aroused instinct propels her to a fateful encounter with Stritch, half starved rock god and member of The Beast's secret cult. Est is inevitably attracted towards the hub of their organisation.

The Beast 666 and his Scarlet Woman 156, luxuriate in ritual sex magick devised to attract new acolytes, while Mama Shag uses Ridelands, her country estate, for secret gatherings of the cult's inner circle. Here acolytes are tested and newcomers initiated, proving their allegiance in the mysteries which unfold within the underground chamber.

> 'I want to thank you for the feast you provided with further pages of 'History of Fun'. I am beginning - *just beginning,* to become conscious of the sheer scope and depth of your vision, to say nothing of the subtleties which lurk in almost every line.' - Kenneth Grant

For inquires about this and other magical and thelemic titles visit our websit at www.mandrake.uk.net or call Mogg for a catalogue on (01865) 243671 Fax (01865) 432929 email Mandrake@mandrake.uk.net or write to: PO Box 250, Oxford, OX1 1AP (UK)